INTRODUCING

The
Holocaust

Haim Bresheeth, Stuart Hood and Litza Jansz

Edited by Richard Appignanesi

ICON BOOKS UK   TOTEM BOOKS USA

This edition published in the UK
in 2000 by Icon Books Ltd.,
Grange Road, Duxford,
Cambridge CB2 4QF
email: icon@mistral.co.uk
www.iconbooks.co.uk

Distributed in the UK, Europe,
Canada, South Africa and Asia by the
Penguin Group: Penguin Books Ltd.,
27 Wrights Lane, London W8 5TZ

This edition published in Australia
in 2000 by Allen & Unwin Pty. Ltd.,
PO Box 8500, 9 Atchison Street,
St. Leonards NSW 2065

Previously published in the UK and
Australia in 1994 under the title
The Holocaust for Beginners

Reprinted 1995, 1997

First published in the United States
in 1994 by Totem Books
Inquiries to: PO Box 223,
Canal Street Station,
New York, NY 10013

Reprinted 1997

In the United States,
distributed to the trade by
National Book Network Inc.,
4720 Boston Way, Lanham,
Maryland 20706

Printed and bound in Australia
by McPherson's Printing Group, Victoria

The Holocaust is what we call the Nazi attempt to destroy European Jewry. It was part of a vast operation in genocide which, between 1939 and 1945, caused the following deaths:

Jews	Between 5 and 6 million
Soviet prisoners of war	Over 3 million
Soviet civilians	2 million
Polish civilians	Over 1 million
Yugoslav civilians	Over 1 million
Men, women and children with mental and physical deficiencies	70,000
Gypsies	Over 200,000
Political prisoners	Unknown
Resistance fighters	Unknown
Deportees	Unknown
Homosexuals	Unknown

שואה

In Hebrew, the Holocaust is called **Shoah** - a great and terrible wind.

"Holocaust" comes from the Greek. **Holos** means "whole" and **caustos** means "burnt" (as in caustic). Originally, it meant a sacrifice consumed by fire - a burnt offering. It came to mean "a sacrifice on a large scale", and, by the end of the 17th century, "the complete destruction of a large number of persons - a great slaughter or massacre."

The Holocaust is an example of Genocide. "Genocide", which literally means the annihilation of a race, was first used in 1944.

The United Nations Convention of 1948 defines the crime of genocide as "acts committed to destroy in whole or in part a national, ethnical, racial or religous group as such."

There have been many cases of genocide in history. The Spanish conquerors slaughtered the Native Americans; whole peoples like the Caribs disappeared. Following on the colonization of North America, the Native Americans were massacred by the army or settlers.

In modern times there have been numerous genocides. Here are some of them:

1904 - 1905	the annihilation of the Herero people in S.W. Africa by the German settlers and army
1915 - 1916	the Turkish massacre of 1 million Armenians
1965 - 1966	up to 1 million Communists and their families massacred by the Indonesian army
1972	between 1 and 3 million Bengalis massacred by the Pakistan army
1972	100,000 to 150,000 Hutus massacred by the ruling Tutsi tribe in Burundi in West Africa
1975-1979	up to 2 million Cambodians murdered by the Khmer Rouge in Kampuchea
1975 to the present	an estimated 200,000 islanders who wish to be independent massacred by the Indonesian army in East Timor
	the continuing destruction of the Indians of the Brazilian rain forest
	the "ethnic cleansing" in former Yugoslavia

Shoah- the Holocaust - was a case of genocide. It was intended by the Nazis to be "the final solution" of what they saw as "the Jewish problem". The Nazis' stated aim was to make the territories under their control **Judenrein** - cleansed of Jews. It was therefore an extreme case of "racial cleansing".
Its ideological basis was **anti-Semitism**.

Anti-Semitism

The word "anti-Semitism" was invented in 1879 by a German racist called Wilhelm Marr (1818-1904).

But anti-Semitism as a phenomenon was many centuries older. It has its roots in religion.

MURDERERS OF THE LORD

REBELS AND DETESTORS OF GOD

COMPANIONS OF THE DEVIL. NO BETTER THAN HOGS IN THEIR LEWD GROSSNESS AND GLUTTONY.

The "Guilt" of the Jews

In the Middle Ages it was an unquestioned part of Christian doctrine that the Jews were guilty of the death of Christ.

They were therefore liable to be massacred at times of Christian fervour.

In 1096 the armies of the First Crusade set out from Western Europe to rescue the holy places of Christianity from their Arab conquerors.

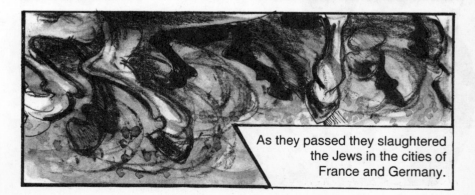

As they passed they slaughtered the Jews in the cities of France and Germany.

Protestant Anti-Semitism

The Protestant church inherited the anti-Semitism of the Catholics. Martin Luther, the great reformer, denounced the Jews as "the devil's people", as "liars and bloodhounds" and "a bloody and revengeful people".

We are at fault in not slaying them. Set fire to their synagogues and schools and bury or cover with dirt whatever will not burn... This is to be done in honour of our Lord and of Christendom, so that God may see that we are Christians.

The Other

Communities tend to define some group or its representative as "the Other". "The Other" is a figure on to whom they project their fears and aggressions. This occurs particularly at times when the community is threatened economically, physically or culturally. "The Other" is usually different in some very obvious ways - skin colour, culture, dress or cuisine and "race" or nationality.

In Christian medieval Europe difference was forced upon the Jews. They were required to live in ghetto segregation.They were said to have a special smell - **foetor Judaicus** - just as other immigrants today are accused of having a "bad smell". Throughout the centuries in Europe, the Jew has been "the Other" - different - set apart - by culture, by religion, by rituals, by dress (in some cases they were compelled to wear badges or specific robes), and by language. Many Jews have - as is their right - held very tenaciously to their differences.

THE RIGHTS OF MAN
LIBERTY
EQUALITY
FRATERNITY
A VINDICATION OF THE RIGHTS OF WOMAN

In the 18th century,
the intellectual movement
known as the **Enlightenment**
produced the body of thought that led to the French Revolution.
It believed in equality irrespective of race.
It was against superstition. All religions, including Christianity and
Judaism, were viewed with equal scepticism. The important thing
was human understanding and tolerance.

As a result of the Enlightenment, the 19th century was a period of assimilation when Jews were received into Gentile society.

WE GAVE OUR BEST TO ART, MUSIC, LITERATURE AND SCIENCE.

WE BECAME PROMINENT IN THE PROFESSIONS AND ACTIVE IN INDUSTRY AND COMMERCE.

But the success of the Jews in these various fields led
to envy and criticism. Jewish entrepreneurs were seen
as "new men" who exploited Jewish family and social
networks (which extended across frontiers)
to further their businesses
in underhand and
unfair ways

> THE JEWS HAD DEVELOPED
> INTO A BOURGEOIS PEOPLE
> WHILE STILL IN THE GHETTO -
> AND THEY STEPPED OUT OF
> IT ONLY TO ENTER INTO
> FIERCE COMPETITION WITH
> THE MIDDLE CLASSES.

Theodor
Herzl
(1860-1904),
the founder
of Zionism

At the same time, Jews became increasingly associated with
liberalism, radicalism, socialism and communism.

The idea took root in anti-Semitic circles that to do away with the
Jews would at one fell swoop do away with capitalism *and*
socialism.

"Scientific" Anti-Semitism

In 1835, Joseph-Arthur Gobineau (1816-1882), a French diplomat, published an influential essay on **The Inequality of the Human Races.**

I BELIEVE THAT THE ARYAN RACE - WHITE EUROPEANS OF THE BLOND NORDIC TYPE - ARE A SUPERIOR RACE.

The Jews were Semites and not Aryans. They therefore constituted a foreign "Oriental" element in European "Aryan" society. They were seen as being unproductive - that is to say not labourers or peasants and yet successful, particularly in commerce and banking, and powerful through their manipulation of the press, the stage and entertainment. Aryans, by contrast, were rooted in **nationhood**.

Jews were believed particularly dangerous, because when they did assimilate, even to the point of abandoning their religion and intermarrying with Christians, they were often difficult to identify - a potential and secret threat to the "race" with which they interbred.

Eugenics

Eugenics was invented by the British scientist Sir Francis Galton (1822-1911). It derived from Darwin's theory of the "survival of the fittest", and argued that society should discourage breeding by those of its members who were "unfit" either physically, mentally or socially.

In 1910, Winston Churchill, as Home Secretary, drafted a proposal to sterilize, or put in labour camps, 100,000 "degenerate British citizens".

In Germany, in 1904, the theory of eugenics was carried to its logical conclusion.

"MERCY DEATH" IS A HYGIENIC WAY TO ELIMINATE THE UNFIT, WHO THUS CEASE TO BE A BURDEN ON SOCIETY.

In 1920, a book was published entitled **The Release and Destruction of Lives Devoid of Value**. Its authors - a lawyer and a psychiatrist proposed euthanasia, enforced by the state, for defective, worthless human beings and those who "represent a foreign body in human society." This is precisely how anti-Semitism defines the Jews.

Ernst Haeckel (1834-1919), German scientist and philosopher

When the Nazis came to power in 1933, they set up a special unit, euphemistically called the **General Foundation for Welfare and Institutional Care**,or T-4.

Made up of doctors and psychiatrists, it carried out "mercy killings" of 70,000 men, women and children in institutions before the programme was officially stopped as a result of protests from clergymen.

The Politics of Anti-Semitism

Towards the end of the 19th century, anti-Semitism began
to take on specifically political forms.

In Germany and Austria, the 1870s had been
a period of severe economic depression.
The lower middle classes - caught
between powerful economic interests
and the rising working-class movement
were particularly affected. A number
of small rightwing groups in Germany
and Austria attacked the Jews,
who at one and the same time
contrived to represent to them
capitalism and radical socialism.

In France, anti-Semitism was, if anything, stronger than in Germany or Austria. French anti-Semitism was traditionally voiced by the Monarchists and the Catholic clergy, both of whom rejected the legacy of the Revolution of 1789 with its motto of **Liberty, Equality and Fraternity**.

ONE UNDESIRABLE EFFECT OF REVOLUTION HAS BEEN THE EMANCIPATION OF THE JEWS!

In the 1890s, the trial and imprisonment of a Jewish officer, Captain Alfred Dreyfus, falsely accused of spying for Germany, revealed the depth of anti-Semitic feeling. The radicals and the Left rose in his defence. The country was split down the middle.

Action Française

After the Dreyfus affair Charles Maurras (1868-1952) a rightwing intellectual, Monarchist and anti-Semite, set up **Action Française** - a seedbed of fascism.

Political parties with anti-Semitic policies, like those in pre-1914 Germany and Austria, were small and relatively unimportant elements in the political spectrum. But they were the forerunners of the **National Socialist German Workers Party** (Nazis) which Hitler formed in the 1920s. This too started as a small party.

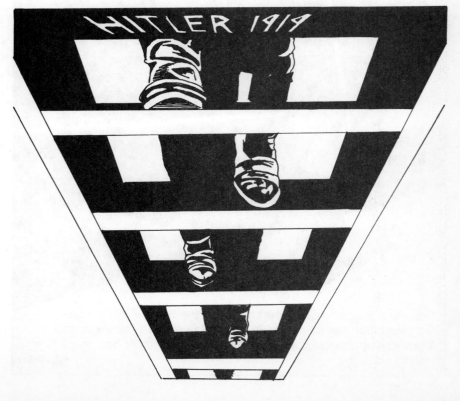

In **Mein Kampf (My Struggle)**, which Hitler wrote in the early 1920s he explained the importance of "racial purity".

"No boy or girl must leave school without having a clear insight into the meaning of racial purity and the importance of maintaining the racial blood unadulterated"

The same racist doctrine was spelt out in the programme of the Nazi party.

Only nationals, it said, can be citizens of the State. Only persons of German blood can be nationals. Jews do not have German blood. Therefore no Jew can become a German national. A logic which can lead to genocide.

The Historical Debate

So did Hitler, did the Nazis, **plan** the Holocaust from the moment they took power?
This is a subject on which there is an important debate.

On the one side are those who believe that it was the Nazis' constant and unwavering intention to destroy European Jewry physically. They are called **intentionalists**.

On the other are those who argue that the Holocaust was reached by what has been called a "twisted road", and many forces within the German state as well as outside it helped to bring it about.
They are called **functionalists**..

This book belongs to the second school of thought.

3 Steps to Genocide

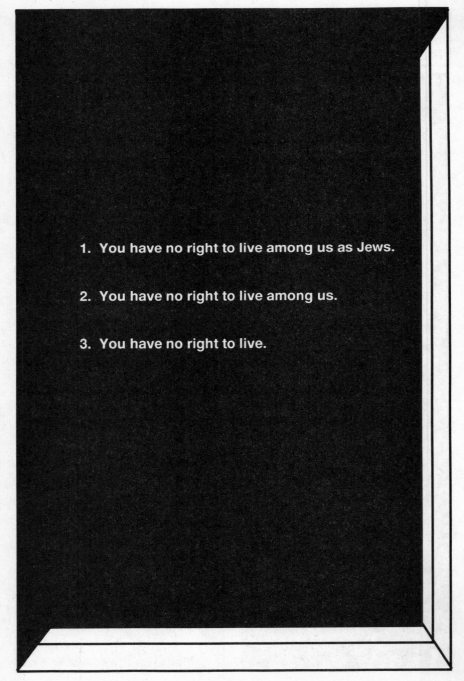

1. You have no right to live among us as Jews.

2. You have no right to live among us.

3. You have no right to live.

How each step came about....

The eminent historian of the Holocaust, Raul Hilberg, summed up in 3 steps the centuries it took to build the railway to genocide. The attentive reader will already have observed how these "steps" came into existence.

First step: the process begins with Christianity's **ghettoization** of the Jews after failing to convert them.

Second step: the process continues in secular Europe when the Jews emerge from the ghetto and are perceived as an **economic threat**, for which reason liberal assimilation fails.

Third step: the Final Solution arrives with the **"scientific"** theory of the Jews as not only racially inferior, but as a menace to the purity of "Aryan" blood.

"The German Nazis, then, did not discard the past; they built on it. They did not begin a development; they completed it. In the deep recesses of anti-Jewish history we shall find many of the administrative and psychological tools with which the Nazis implemented their destruction process. In the hollows of the past we shall also discover the roots of the characteristic Jewish response to an outside attack."

Raul Hilberg
The Destruction of the European Jews

The Nazis came to power in 1933, with the blessing and support of the German Right, the German industrialists and the German army.

WE CAN USE HITLER TO RID US OF THE TRADE UNIONS!

AND MAKE GERMANY SAFE FOR CAPITALISM.

The German parliament immediately passed an Act granting Hitler dictatorial powers. The rightwing and centre parties voted for the Act. Only the socialists and communists dared to vote against the measures.

Concentration
camps had been
invented by the
British in the
Boer War for the
internment of Boer men,
women and children.
Concentrated - that is to
say, forcibly collected and
interned in these camps.
They died in great
numbers from neglect and
disease.

Hitler then began a reign of terror
against his political opponents.
Communists, socialists, radicals,
trade unionists - there were plenty of
Jews among them!
They were imprisoned without trial in
concentration camps -
Konzentrationslager (KZ).

MADE IN

ENGLAND

The first German concentration camp was set up at Dachau in March 1933 - less than two months after Hitler came to power. From the start the German KZs adopted brutal penal methods - hard labour, floggings, executions.

Camps at Dachau, Sachsen Hausen and Buchenwald held some 50,000 prisoners between them, half of them being "asocial" elements to be used for forced labour.

The Segregation Programme Is Applied.

On coming to power, the Nazis at once set about introducing a series of laws which aimed to exclude "non-Aryans", i.e. Jews, from public life. "Non-Aryans" were defined as persons with a Jewish parent or grandparent.

Having begun with the Civil Service, the Nazis went on to banish Jews from teaching in schools and universities and set a quota on Jewish students. Jews were barred from practising as doctors, dentists and judges. They might not sit as jurors. They were declared ineligible for military service.

"Aryanization" of cultural institutions meant that Jews were excluded from cultural life. They were forbidden to be publishers or editors.

Jews who had been naturalized after 1918 - they were mostly from Eastern Europe - lost their citizenship. As a result they became in effect **stateless**.

Humiliating legislation forbade Jews from owning dogs or using public parks, swimming pools or spas. Those measures were widely accepted by the majority of the German public, despite the intense criticisism voiced abroad.

This was apartheid.

The Nuremberg Laws

The original definition of a 'non-Aryan' did not satisfy the racial purists in the Nazi party. There were also problems about the classification of 'non-Aryans' for administrative and bureaucratic purposes.

During the famous Nuremberg Rally of 1935, Hitler gave orders that a *Law for the Protection of German Blood and Honour* should be drawn up in the space of two days. "Experts" from the Ministry of the Interior produced the legislation with almost ludicrous haste.
The resulting decrees came to be known as the Nuremberg Laws.

HOW DO I KNOW THEY'RE NOT ALL JEWISH?

The Nuremberg Laws began by asserting that only a person of German "or related " blood could be a German citizen. Jews were therefore deprived of German citizenship.

A Jew was a person defined partly by race and partly by religion. Thus a person was considered a Jew if he or she was descended from at least three grandparents who were Jewish by race, or from two grandparents who belonged to the Jewish religion or had married a Jewish person.

The experts also invented another category. These were the so-called **Mischlinge** (persons of mixed descent) who had one or two grandparents who were Jewish by race but did not subscribe to the Jewish religion. Mischlinge were subject to discrimination and were also at risk of worse, but less so than full Jews.

There was thus a three-tiered system with the "Aryans" at the top, the Mischlinge in the middle, and the Jews at the bottom of the pile.

The Laws also forbade marriage and sexual relations between Jews and non-Jews. These offences were to be punished by imprisonment. Jews were not to employ in their homes females of German or related blood under the age of 45.

Economic Aryanization

Immediately on coming to power in 1933, Hitler sanctioned a one-day boycott of Jewish shops and businesses to appease the radicals in the Nazi party.

NOT A SUCCESS, BECAUSE MOST ORDINARY GERMANS AREN'T ACTIVELY ANTI-SEMITIC.

YES IT IS - BECAUSE IT ESTABLISHES THAT JEWS CAN'T HOPE TO BE PROTECTED BY THE LAW LIKE OTHER CITIZENS!

In spite of the difficulties placed in their way, many Jewish firms remained in business. But in 1937, a series of decrees "aryanized" Jewish concerns. Jews were required to sell or liquidate their businesses at ridiculous prices. "Aryan" capitalists cashed in.

Exodus

There were half-a-million Jews in the **Third Reich** at the Nazi coming to power in 1933. The result of Nazi oppression and the anti-Jewish legislation was a series of waves of emigration.

The first main wave was between 1933 and 1936.

> MANY OF US EMIGRATED TO NEIGHBOURING COUNTRIES, LIKE FRANCE.
> THREE QUARTERS STAYED IN EUROPE. ONE FIFTH WENT TO PALESTINE.

The second wave came after the **Anschluss** - the Nazi takeover of Austria - in March 1938. This brought another 180,000 Jews under Nazi rule - and a mass flight of Jews from Austria. To control it, an Office of Emigration was set up in Vienna. It was run by a low-ranking SS officer called Adolf Eichmann (1906-executed 1962).

The third wave followed the **Kristallnacht** - the night of broken glass.

The Night of Broken Glass

In October 1938, 15,000 Polish Jews were expelled from Germany and dumped at the Polish border. The rightwing anti-Semitic Polish government, which was talking about its own "Jewish problem", refused them entry.

In revenge, a young Polish Jew, whose parents had been expelled, shot an official at the German Embassy in Paris. The Nazi Party said it was part of a world-wide Jewish conspiracy, and on 9/10 November, responded with a night of brutality, arson, murder. Some 300 synagogues were burned. At least 7,000 shops were destroyed and looted. Jewish cemeteries were desecrated. 91 Jews were killed.

Jews were arrested in large numbers and taken to the concentration camps. Most of them were released by the end of the year, but 1,000 had been killed.

A "Jewish Atonement Fine" was imposed for the damage caused. It had the effect of stripping the remaining Jews of most of their assets. The Jews were by now effectively excluded from German economic life.

The Kristallnacht - the Night of Broken Glass - was the work of the brownshirted SA: the uniformed Nazis, the radicals of the party. It did not please Hitler because it was not carried out under the central control of the regime.

THERE MUST BE A METHODICALLY PLANNED APPROACH TO THE JEWISH QUESTION WITHIN A BUREAUCRATIC FRAMEWORK.

The Role of the SS

The SS played a crucial part in formulating and implementing Hitler's policy.

The SS began as Hitler's bodyguard (**Schutzstaffel**). They were a racial elite who had to provide evidence of Aryan ancestry. They swore absolute loyalty to Hitler. SS troops not only ran and guarded the concentration camps, but also put infantry and armoured divisions into the field.

The head of the SS was Heinrich Himmler (1900-committed suicide May 1945), one of the most powerful men in Nazi Germany. He had under him the **Reich Security Main Office** (RHSA), run by Rudolf Heydrich (born 1904-assassinated 1942). The Gestapo (secret police) and the security services were also under Himmler's command.

POLICY

Heydrich applied the ideology of anti-Semitism with cold logic that led eventually to the Final Solution.

Making the Reich "Judenrein"

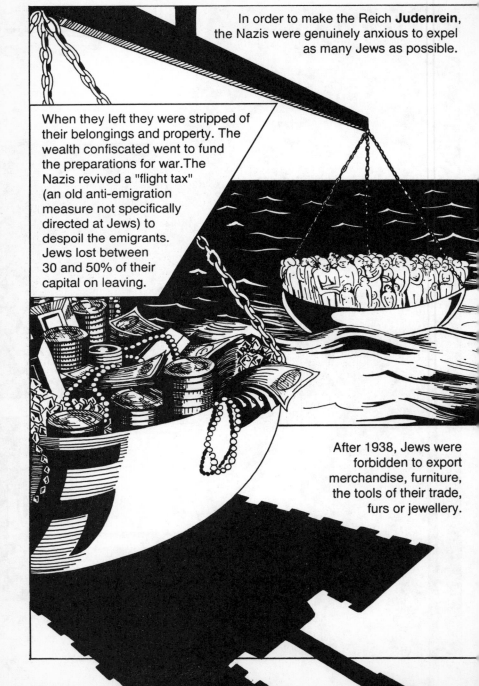

In order to make the Reich **Judenrein**, the Nazis were genuinely anxious to expel as many Jews as possible.

When they left they were stripped of their belongings and property. The wealth confiscated went to fund the preparations for war. The Nazis revived a "flight tax" (an old anti-emigration measure not specifically directed at Jews) to despoil the emigrants. Jews lost between 30 and 50% of their capital on leaving.

After 1938, Jews were forbidden to export merchandise, furniture, the tools of their trade, furs or jewellery.

The Nazis' desire to get rid of Jews from the Reich coincided with the Zionist wish to encourage emigration to Palestine. A transfer agreement (**Ha'avara**) was therefore reached between the 3rd Reich and the Zionist Federation in Palestine,whereby Jews could move part of their capital to Palestine in the form of German goods.This agreement did not find favour with some Jewish organizations. Chief among these was the **World Jewish Congress** (WJC) which had organized a boycott of all German goods.
This agreement undermined the boycott.

In all, about one-half of the 500,000 German and the 200,000 Austrian Jews contrived to emigrate wherever they could.

The world refugee problem, already grave because of economic depression and large scale unemployment, became worse in the late 30s owing to the numbers escaping from fascism in Spain, in Italy and the German Reich.

Of the latter, many - but not all - were Jews. As the Nazis pursued their policy of making the Reich "Judenrein", the number of refugees naturally swelled. They were becoming desperate.

The United Kingdom had no quota system, but the government declared that it was not "a country of immigration".

In Britain, enlightened opinion and organizations - both Jewish and non-Jewish - were active in helping refugees from Nazism. To ease access, the Anglo-Jewish community made a promise. Jewish refugees would not become a financial burden to the State.

YES, BUT THIS WILL MAKE IT DIFFICULT FOR UNSPONSORED PERSONS TO GAIN ADMITTANCE.

By the outbreak of war in September 1939, 80,000 refugees had been admitted. They included some 10,000 children who arrived after the Kristallnacht; 70% of them were Jewish.

43

The British Mandate

Zionists naturally favoured Palestine, where there were already nearly 200,000 Jewish settlers. As part of the post-World War I settlement, Palestine was held by Britain as a mandate until the country was judged ready for independence. To win their support in the war, the British government had made contradictory promises to the indigenous Arabs and to the Jewish settlers.

WE HELPED THE ARABS TO WIN INDEPENDENCE FROM THE TURKISH EMPIRE.

ON THE OTHER HAND, IN 1917 WE PROMISED A JEWISH HOMELAND IN PALESTINE, WITHOUT TAKING INTO ACCOUNT THE WISHES AND NEEDS OF THE ARAB POPULATION.

T.E. LAWRENCE

BRITISH LIES PROMISES

Although openly anti-Semitic, the Colonial Office allowed Jews to emigrate to Palestine in almost unrestricted numbers until 1936.
At the peak of prewar Nazi persecution, a royal commision recommended that Jewish immigration be limited to a maximum of 12,000 per annum for 5 years.
In May 1939, the British government revised this to a total of 75,000 - thereafter there would be no admittance without Arab consent.

This led to large scale illegal immigration, whereby between 1938 and 1941 over 18,000 Jews entered Palestine. The British reaction was fierce and often brutal.

THE EVIAN

In July 1938, 33 governments attended a conference in the pleasant French spa of Evian to discuss the refugee situation. The Third Reich was represented by five SS officers.

CONFERENCE

NO GOVERNMENT WILL BE EXPECTED TO RECEIVE A GREATER NUMBER OF EMIGRANTS THAN IS PERMITTED BY EXISTING LEGISLATION. FINANCE WILL COME FROM PRIVATE SOURCES.

The invitation to attend came from the American government.

It was clear to the Jewish organizations present at Evian - although not participants in the conference - that...

THERE'S NO HOPE OF MORE LIBERAL IMMIGRATION POLICIES.

ALL WE CAN FEEL IS SORROW, RAGE, FRUSTRATION AND HORROR!

Suppose the conference does actually find territories other than Palestine to shelter Jewish refugees? If other doors are open, it will cause untold damage to Zionism in Palestine! Better the conference comes to no decision.

David Ben-Gurion (1886-1973) future Prime Minister of Israel

EVIAN

I can only hope that the other world which has such deep sympathy for these criminals will at least be generous enough to convert this sympathy into practical aid.

We are ready to put all these criminals at the disposal of these countries... even on luxury ships.

War was now looming.

In January 1939, speaking to the German parliament, Hitler prophesied that...

IF THE INTERNATIONAL JEWISH
FINANCIERS IN AND OUTSIDE
EUROPE
SHOULD SUCCEED IN PLUNGING
THE NATIONS ONCE MORE INTO
A WORLD WAR,
THEN THE RESULT WILL BE NOT
THE BOLSHEVIZATION OF THE
EARTH
AND THUS
THE VICTORY OF JEWRY
BUT THE ANNIHILATION OF
THE JEWISH RACE
IN EUROPE.

The question is: To what extent was this a statement of policy. Or mere rhetoric, in an attempt to blackmail world opinion?

Europe under Nazi Occupation

By the summer of 1940, German-occupied territory in Europe stretched from the Bay of Biscay to central Poland.

For the Jews in that territory, there was no longer any question of being able to emigrate in large numbers. But, as yet, the Nazis seem not to have had any clear idea of how to make it **Judenrein**. Thus, in 1940, they were discussing a plan - warmly welcomed by Heydrich...

The plan was not finally buried until 1941. As an interim solution, the Jews of the conquered territories in Europe were shipped to German-controlled territory in Poland...

51

The Jews of Poland

Even before the Jews from occupied Europe arrived in Poland, 10% of the population was Jewish. The Polish Jewish community had settled in the 14th century, at the invitation of the Polish kings.

> We were the king's tax-gatherers. Where we settled was known as the Pale of Settlement.

The Pale, extending into the Ukraine, became a great centre of Jewish society and culture. Some 8 million Jews lived between the Baltic and the Black Seas. Anti-Semitism was endemic there.

How to De-humanize a Population

With the German occupation of Poland in September 1939, the old pattern of pogrom and anti-Semitic abuse was encouraged by the Nazis.

New decrees were published almost daily, limiting the freedom and activities of the Jewish population. Jews could not use a tram without a delousing certificate, renewable weekly. All Jews had to salute all Nazi personnel. They had to wear the yellow star at all times.

A series of "games" were invented by the Nazi, who took special delight in humiliating the spiritual leadership.

A rabbi snatched from a restaurant and forced to clear snow was then forced to shit in his pants. Groups of Jewish workers were made to fight each other at gunpoint. Jews were thrown out of tramcars, and forced to clean toilets with bare hands. Cases of madness multiplied, partly as a result of the large number of beatings and head injuries.

Most Poles acquiesced in the atrocities, though they may not have participated in them. But an important minority assisted the Jews - warning them, for instance, of the approach of press-gangs.

In September 1939, Heydrich, as head of the Reich Security Main Office, issued a directive on "the Jewish question in the occupied territory of Poland".

JEWS ARE TO BE TAKEN FROM THE COUNTRYSIDE AND PLACED IN THE LARGER CITIES AT RAILWAY JUNCTIONS OR ON RAILWAY LINES

THE 'FINAL AIM' IS TO BE KEPT STRICTLY SECRET AND NOT DEFINED.

IN EACH JEWISH COMMUNITY A COUNCIL OF JEWISH ELDERS IS TO BE SET UP AND MADE FULLY RESPONSIBLE FOR THE IMPLEMENTATION OF ALL DIRECTIVES FROM THE NAZIS

The Ghettos

The next step was the setting up of ghettos.

In the Middle Ages, most European Jews were forced to live in ghettos separate from the Christian population. It was only during the 18th century that full emancipation was granted to Jews, although the old mechanisms of racial control did not disappear.

REVERSION TO THE GHETTO MEANT THE LOSS OF ALL ADVANTAGES OF LIBERAL DEMOCRACY, WON AFTER LONG, HARD STRUGGLE.

Ghettoization under the Nazis was a gradual process. The first main ghetto was set up in Lodz in April 1940. The Warsaw ghetto was not created until October of that year. Those in Krakow and Lublin were established in 1941.

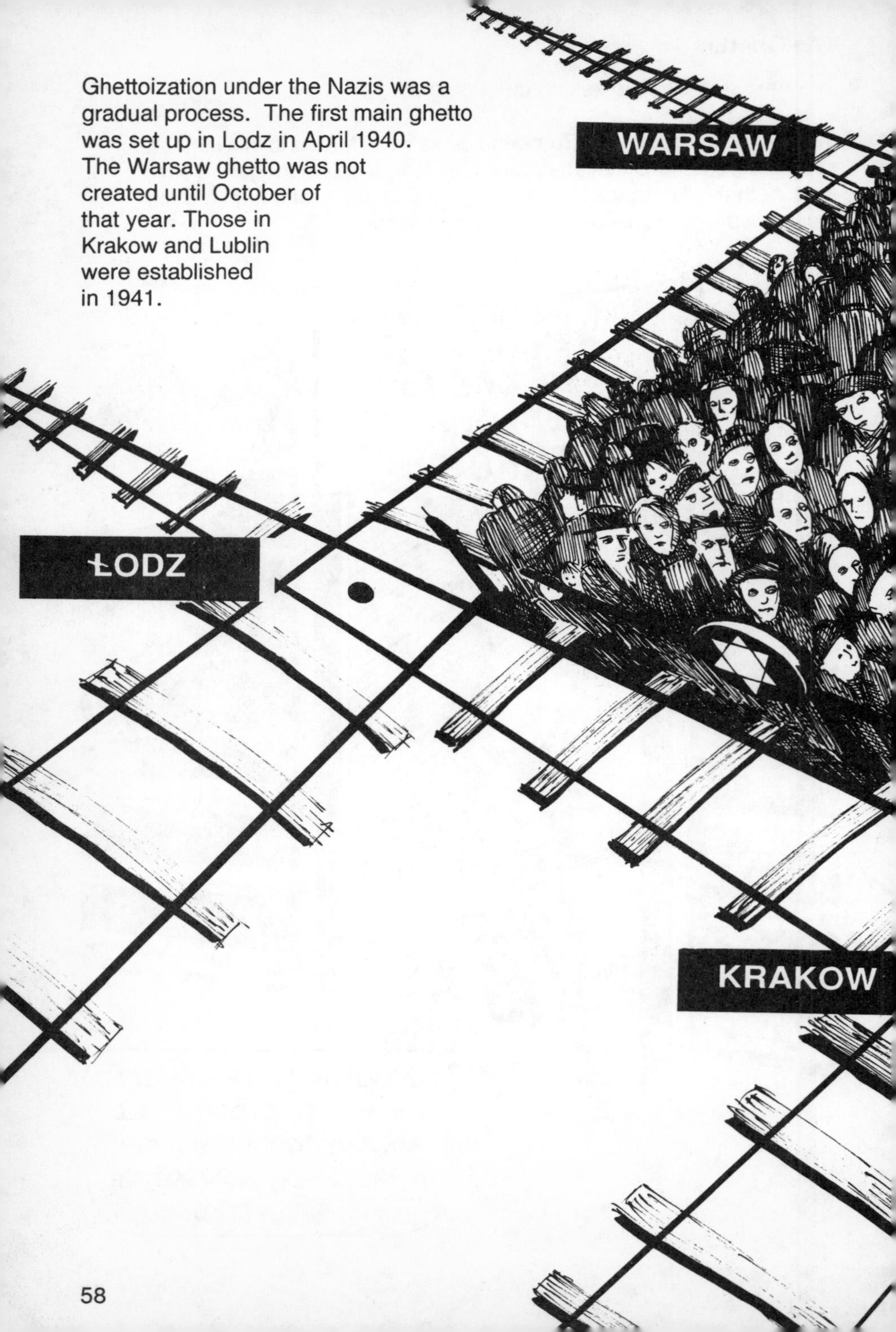

WARSAW

ŁODZ

KRAKOW

At first the ghettos gave a false sense of security.

THERE'S LESS INTIMIDATION BECAUSE THERE'S NO DIRECT CONTACT BETWEEN US AND THE GENTILE POPULATION.

LUBLIN

THE NUMBER OF SUICIDES HAVE FALLEN.

But the ghettos also marked the Jews as people who were **different**, living in squalid conditions, wracked by disease. The result was to **dehumanize** them in the eyes of society outside the ghetto.

The business of setting up the ghettos and appointing the Councils (**Judenräte**) was entrusted to special security units - the **Einsatzgruppen**.

59

Resistance or Collaboration?

The ghettos have been described as "captive city-states totally subject to the German authorities". Each ghetto had its own administrative body - the Judenrat (Jewish Council).

Sometimes, the Nazis ordered prominent persons to select a Council.Other times, they were selected pretty much arbitrarily.To refuse to serve meant death.Many brave men died in this way.

The Councils were overwhelmingly middle class: merchants and professional men - doctors, dentists, lawyers, etc.

In some ghettos there was opposition to the establishment of the Councils by the Jewish community and calls for a boycott. The question was: Would the councils make it easier for the Germans to persecute the Jews, or would they be able to cushion the effects of persecution?

At first some heads of Councils thought there could be "salvation through work". Lodz became important in supplying the German army with clothing. In the Warsaw ghetto 25,000 Jews were employed on war production.

The policy of "salvation through work" fitted in well with the economic strategy of the SS. In reality the only purpose of the Councils was to carry out the orders of the German authorities.

The Nazi policy was a cunning one. Although the population of the ghettos understood who was responsible for their unbearable conditions, they found themselves being ruled by fellow Jews and confronting their own leaders rather than the hated Nazis.

The Warsaw Ghetto

The Warsaw ghetto was the largest of all.

Almost half a million people, over a third of the population of Warsaw, were crammed into a mere 1.3 square miles. The rest of the population inhabited 53.3 square miles. The average room held over 7 people. Only one percent of the apartments had running water. Only a tenth of the population was allowed to cross into the "Aryan" side to work. All aspects of life in the ghetto were controlled by the Nazis through the Judenrat, which grew enormously from a liaison bureau to a body governing 500,000 people living in the most inhuman conditions.

Since the Jews were completely cut off, the Warsaw Council - like other councils - had to take over the task of providing social services: health care; education; rationing; food distribution; soup kitchens; the organization of the Jewish ghetto police and the administration of justice; hospitals and sanitation; burials; culture (Jews were forbidden to play music by "Aryan" composers). It also organized the industry in the ghetto in which half the population toiled.

The leader of the Warsaw Judenrat was Adam Czerniakow (1888-1942) who represented the liberal-progressive wing of the ghetto leadership.

Like all Judenrat leaders, Czerniakow built up industrial production as an insurance policy against extermination.

THEY WON'T KILL THE GOOSE THAT LAYS THE GOLDEN EGGS.

Ghetto industries created a new elite who owned and ran the workshops and plants.

In cases like that, the Judenrat majority appealed to the Nazi authorities, who sided with it and created conflict within the Council.

Because of starvation and disease, the death rate in the ghetto was terrifying. Typhoid and dysentery killed large numbers every week. Those who survived were so weak that they were unable to work, and thus became an economic burden.

I DID MY BEST TO PROTECT THE WEAKEST, DESPITE INTERNAL OPPOSITION, AND WITH LIMITED SUCCESS. THE WEAK WERE CANDIDATES FOR "RESETTLEMENT" - WHICH MEANT LIQUIDATION.

By July 1942, over 100,000 Jews had already perished because of conditions inside the ghetto, leaving 380,000 survivors.

When the Nazis demanded that the Judenrat should supply 10,000 non-productive Jews a day for "resettlement", Czerniakow inquired how long the deportations would continue. The Nazi reply was: "Seven days a week, until the end".

When Czerniakow saw that they intended to exterminate everyone in the ghetto, he committed suicide.

The remaining members of the Judenrat believed that a substantial number would be allowed to go on producing. They therefore vetoed any organized resistance to the deportations, which continued at the pace of 10,000 a day. By September, there were only 70,000 Jews left in the ghetto. They would be destroyed in 1943 during and after the Warsaw Ghetto rising.

In Lodz, the Judenrat leader, Mordecai Rumkowski (1877-1942), was known to the Jews as "the king". He organized the ghetto - population about 180,000 - with efficiency and tyrannical rigour. When the deportations began in mid-1942, he adopted the deliberate policy of "sacrificing the few to save the many". In other words, he decided who was to die and who was to live. When the Soviet troops took Lodz in August 1944, there were only 870 survivors. Rumkowski, along with most of the inhabitants, had been despatched to the gas chambers.

In Vilna, the head of the Judenrat was Jacob Gens, an ex-officer in the Lithuanian army. He believed that salvation lay in labour, law and order.
His policy was clear.

WHEN THE GERMANS COME AND ASK FOR 1,000 PEOPLE I PROVIDE THEM, FOR IF WE JEWS DO NOT PROVIDE THEM OF OUR OWN FREE WILL... THE WHOLE GHETTO WILL BE IN DANGER.

He knew his hands were dirty and bloody, but "I did everything in my power to save Jews."

Although he basically opposed armed resistance, Gens was shot by the Gestapo, a few days before the ghetto was liquidated, for having contacts with the partisans.

It was the tragedy of such men that once the Nazis had decided on the "Final Solution to the Jewish question", they were inextricably caught in a process that led step by step to the destruction of the ghetto inmates. There was an inescapable progression from providing a census of Jews, to detailing them for forced labour and, eventually, to deciding who should be deported to die in the camps. The **Judenräte** were, if unwillingly and unwittingly, an enabling device in the great extermination machine, smoothing its complex operations.

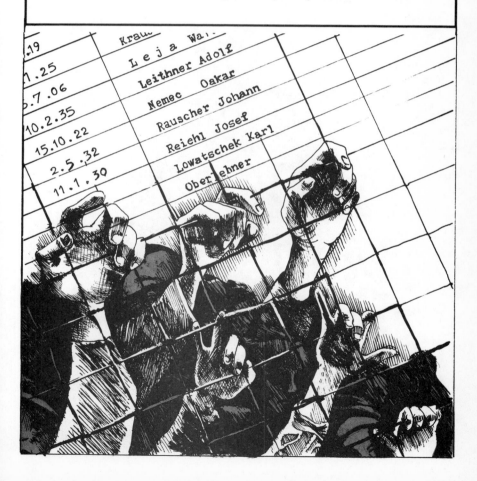

The Invasion of Russia and the *Endlösung*

The decision to move towards the "Final Solution to the Jewish question" was taken after the invasion of the Soviet Union in 1941. This was an ideological war directed not only against the "subhuman" Slavs, but also the "subhuman" Jews. Field Marshal von Reichnau declared in an order of the day:

> In the Eastern sphere the soldier is not simply a fighter according to the rules of war but the supporter of a ruthless racial ideology... for this reason the soldier must show full understanding of the necessity of the severe but just atonement being required of the Jewish sub-humans.

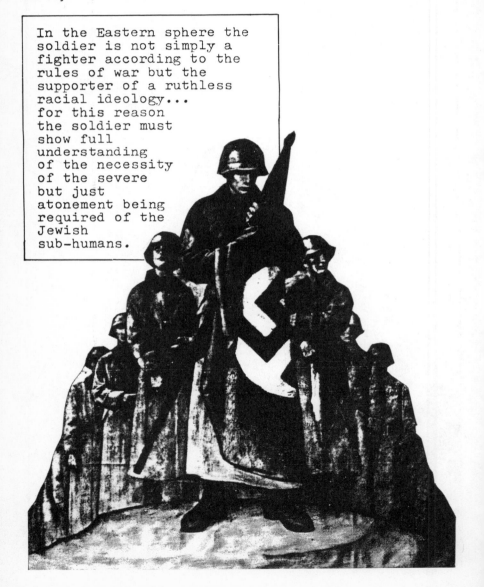

In July 1941- a month after the invasion of the Soviet Union - Hermann Goering (1893-1946) - Hitler's second in command and presumably acting in line with the intentions of the Fuehrer signed an order, drafted by Heydrich.

YOU ARE INSTRUCTED TO MAKE ALL NECESSARY PREPARATIONS FOR A TOTAL SOLUTION OF THE JEWISH QUESTION.

The *Endlösung* - the Final Solution.

At the beginning of July, Heydrich gave special orders for the conquered territories of the Soviet Union.

NOT ONLY ALL COMMUNIST OFFICIALS ARE TO BE EXECUTED, BUT ALL JEWS IN PARTY AND STATE EMPLOYMENT, ALONG WITH SABOTEURS, SNIPERS, PROPAGANDISTS, ASSASSINS, INCITERS, ETC. - THAT IS, PARTISANS.

This was the task of **Einsatzgruppen** - murder squads - who moved into captured towns and localities with the forward troops. It soon became clear that they took Heydrich to mean that *all* Jews - including women and children - should be killed.

The Massacres Begin

The massacres carried out by the Einsatzgruppen might be called the "primitive phase" of the Final Solution. These units were **not** made up of criminals, sadists and maniacs, but were drawn from the elite of the German professional middle class.

One was a Protestant minister. There were more PhD graduates among them proportionally than in any other unit of the German army. They were hand-picked for strong ideological motivation and reliability.

There were only four Einsatzgruppen battalions for the whole of the huge Russian front, from the Baltic to the Black Sea.

Reinforced by Security Police units, and helped by German army units, they moved into conquered territory and set to work massacring whole Jewish communities. The **local population** frequently joined in as auxiliary police, especially in the Baltic states and the Ukraine, assisting the roundups with their local knowledge. They were rewarded with the pick of the property of the dead Jews.

The squads had a standard technique

- A mass grave was found or dug outside a locality.

- The Jews were ordered to an assembly point.

- They were taken in batches (men first) to the killing area.

- They handed over any valuables to the commander of the squad.

- They removed their outer clothing and, in summer, stripped bare.

- They were killed on the edge of the grave by single shots or massed fire.

The first massacres of Jews took place as the German armies entered the Baltic states and the Ukraine. In **Kovno**: Lithuanian 'partisans' killed some 8,000 Jews. In Lvov: Ukrainian nationalists killed 7,000. But the Einsatzgruppen were responsible for the bulk of the killings. In **Kiev**, two days, 33,000 Jews were killed in a ravine called Babi Yar.

As the front moved east the squads found fewer victims. The Jews had fled eastwards or been evacuated by the Russians. A million and a half Jews were saved in this way.

Germany's ally Romania was also zealous. In **Odessa**, the city with the largest Jewish population in the Soviet Union, the Romanian army shot or burned some 40,000 Jews as a reprisal for a partisan attack.

The civilian and Christian population was at best passive during these and other atrocities. In Lithuania, for instance, a bishop forbade the clergy to aid Jews or intercede for them in any way.

In October 1941, one Einsatzgruppe reported that it had killed 125,000 Jews and gave the exact numbers per community, with a statistical break-down of men and women, and also of Communists.

Psychological Problem

It became clear that the methods of the Einsatzgruppen were inappropriate for dealing with the huge numbers involved. The *methods* also placed a strain on those doing the killing. Himmler later referred to the "psychological problem" in a secret speech to Police Generals in Poland.

MOST OF YOU MUST KNOW WHAT IT MEANS WHEN ONE HUNDRED CORPSES ARE LYING SIDE BY SIDE, OR FIVE HUNDRED, OR ONE THOUSAND. TO HAVE STUCK IT OUT, AND AT THE SAME TIME - APART FROM EXCEPTIONS CAUSED BY HUMAN WEAKNESS - TO HAVE REMAINED DECENT FELLOWS, THAT IS WHAT HAS MADE US HARD. THIS IS A PAGE OF GLORY IN OUR HISTORY WHICH IS NEVER TO BE WRITTEN...

Himmler - as he told
an SS Police General -
saw a solution to the
psychological problem
n new techniques
which would make the
killings more
mpersonal.

"For executions by
shooting you need
people who can do the
shooting and it has a
bad effect on them.
So it would be better to
iquidate human
beings by using
'gas-vans' which have
been prepared to my
specifications in
Germany. By their use
he unpleasantnesses
connected with
execution by shooting
are removed."

The Gas Vans

Himmler was referring to Mobile Gas Vans in use at the Chelmno extermination camp. Carbon monoxide from the vans' exhaust-pipes were pumped into the sealed load space, killing up to 40 persons in one operation.

The mobile gas vans were designed for a typical trip of about ten miles from the loading point to the burial trenches. This meant that the drivers had to drive at a speed not exceeding 20 mph to allow time for the entrapped Jews to be gassed. But the drivers, despite the large amounts of alcoholic drinks dispensed to them, found the job upsetting and drove faster in order to "get it over with".

As a result, the Jews were not quite dead when the vans arrived at the trenches. The scenes facing the drivers and guards were too much even for men hardened by habitual brutality. Yet between December 1941 and spring 1943, over 200,000 Polish Jews and tens of thousands of Soviet prisoners and gypsies were murdered in this way.

Re: **A Technical Problem**

In Saurer vehicles, maximum use of space is impossible, because loading to full capacity would affect the vehicle's stability. (Load space) must be reduced instead of trying to solve the problem as hitherto by reducing the number of pieces loaded. If the load space is reduced and the vehicle is packed solid the operating time can be considerably shortened. The manufacturers told us that reducing the size of the vehicle's rear would throw it badly off balance. The front axle, they claim, would be overloaded. In fact, the balance is automatically restored, because the merchandise aboard displays during the operation a natural tendency to rush to the rear doors and is mainly found lying there at the end of the operation. So the front axle is not overloaded.

W. Just

Will Just
Welder,
RHSA Transport
Dept.

The Industrialization of Mass Murder

Another important innovation was made at Treblinka. Here, instead of being taken to their deaths in gas vans, the Jews were brought en masse to a purpose-built sealed chamber. The commandant then pumped carbon monoxide from an engine into the chamber, killing the 200 Jews huddled inside within 20-30 minutes. For the first time, Jews were being killed in great numbers *without anyone in particular doing the killing.*

The messy job of pulling the bodies out of the vans and the Treblinka gas chamber was carried out by **Sonderkommandos** - Special Squads - of Jewish inmates, temporarily reprieved for the purpose. The method of corpse disposal remained the same. The bodies were buried in layers in large trenches dug out by mechanical excavators.

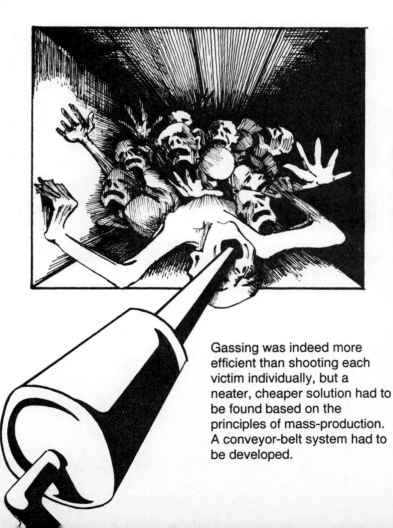

Gassing was indeed more efficient than shooting each victim individually, but a neater, cheaper solution had to be found based on the principles of mass-production. A conveyor-belt system had to be developed.

Programming the Final Solution

In August 1941, SS Chief Himmler gave orders for the preparation of the Auschwitz death camp.

In September 1941, Christian Wirth, SS Head of the T-4 organization and an expert on "mercy killings", was appointed to Chelmno where he proceeded to gas inmates.

In December 1941, Hans Frank (1900-46) Nazi Governor-General of Occupied Poland, announced a big conference for January 1942 in Berlin.

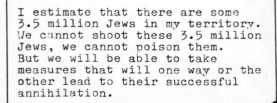

I estimate that there are some 3.5 million Jews in my territory. We cannot shoot these 3.5 million Jews, we cannot poison them. But we will be able to take measures that will one way or the other lead to their successful annihilation.

The conference Governor Frank had talked about took place on 20 January 1942. It was held in a villa at Wannsee on the outskirts of Berlin - with breakfast. The aim of the Conference was to co-ordinate the work of the various agencies that would be involved in the operation of the "Final Solution". Fifteen people took part - a mixture of SS officers and security police, party officials and high civil servants.

If Eichmann, SS Colonel, Chief of Bureau Gestapo Jewish Office, drew up the minutes nference. Its chief points were:

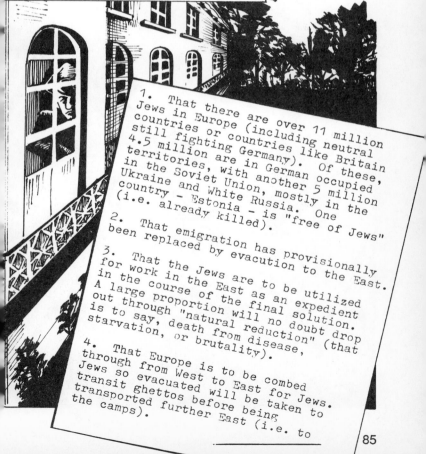

1. That there are over 11 million Jews in Europe (including neutral countries or countries like Britain still fighting Germany). Of these, 4.5 million are in German occupied territories, with another 5 million in the Soviet Union, mostly in the Ukraine and White Russia. One country – Estonia – is "free of Jews" (i.e. already killed).

2. That emigration has provisionally been replaced by evacuation to the East.

3. That the Jews are to be utilized for work in the East as an expedient in the course of the final solution. A large proportion will no doubt drop out through "natural reduction" (that is to say, death from disease, starvation, or brutality).

4. That Europe is to be combed through from West to East for Jews. Jews so evacuated will be taken to transit ghettos before being transported further East (i.e. to the camps).

The Economics of the Final Solution

Wannsee took place at a moment when the German offensive in the East had been halted by tough Russian resistance and the Russian winter. The German Army had suffered immense losses in men and equipment. The need to replace these casualties threatened the German war industry with a manpower shortage.

The answer was for German industry and German agriculture to use forced and slave labour. Some of this would come from the ghettos. The inmates of the concentration camps were also to play their part. A few days after Wannsee, Himmler announced that the concentration camps would receive "great economic contracts and assignments".

"It's Good for Business..."

> When you buy a good horse you have to accept a few shortcomings.
>
> Munitions tycoon Gustav Krupp, on the Nazi system

> At the peak of their employment, something like 500,000 concentration camp inmates were employed in German industry as a whole.
>
> Karl Sommer
> SS Officer in W.V.H.A.

> On the occasion of a dinner given to us by the administration of the concentration camp, we laid down all the measures concerning the activation of the truly splendid plant in the KZ for the benefit of the Buna works.
>
> Dr Otto Ambros, Director of IG Farben, 12 April 1941

This "good business" policy ran counter to the physical extermination of the Jews which was already under way at the hands of the *Einsatzgruppen,* and which from time to time made the German Army complain that a valuable labour force was being depleted. It was a contradiction which would be resolved in favour of ideology and extermination. **In the Third Reich, ideology often won over pragmatism.**

Types of Camps and their Purposes

The new industrial killing techniques were developed in the concentration camps run by the Economic Central Office of the SS (WVHA).

There were three types of camp.

1. **Concentration Camps (KZ)** such as Buchenwald, Bergen-Belsen and others. They were not equipped to kill large numbers of people.

2. **Work Camps** - they ranged from very small camps supplying slave labour for local industries to the huge IG Farben camp at Auschwitz III which employed over 15,000 Jews on average at any time.

3. **Extermination Camps** like Sobibor, Chelmno,
Birkenau and Treblinka. These were specialist units -
industrial killing centres, processing death on a massive scale.
Over 3 million people died in them.

The Killing Centres

The KZ, the gas chamber and the crematorium - all tried and tested - were combined in the killing centres of extermination camps.

The death camps at Auschwitz-Birkenau, Chelmno, Treblinka, Sobibor, Majdanek and Belzec - all in remote parts of Poland - were historically unique. Their sole purpose was the speedy and cost effective production of mass death, including the processing of the by-products, and the total elimination of all evidence of the extermination process. Here Jews (referred to as **Stücke** ,"pieces") were to be "processed" within less than six hours, and sometimes in under an hour, from their arrival by train.

The camps were built as production-line units to run without delays or hitches. Most of the main extermination camps operated from 1941 to the end of 1944.

While Chelmno continued to use the outdated gas vans, all the rest used specially built gas chambers, mostly operating with carbon monoxide. Auschwitz alone, the most modern and largest complex, was equipped with a superior method of killing: the deadly crystals known commercially as Zyklon B-hydrogen cyanide, or prussic acid.

The Transports

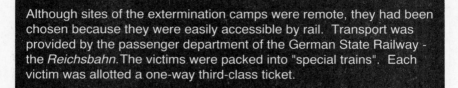

Although sites of the extermination camps were remote, they had been chosen because they were easily accessible by rail. Transport was provided by the passenger department of the German State Railway - the *Reichsbahn.* The victims were packed into "special trains". Each victim was allotted a one-way third-class ticket.

Children under 10 travel half-fare.

Infants travel free.

Group fares available if the number transported is more than 300.

Each transport delivered between 1,200 and 3,000 Jews. Of these, some 10% of the men and 5% of the women were selected for work. The rest were made to run through lines of SS "helpers" with dogs, to the undressing block, where they were stripped of their possessions and were shaved by inmate barbers. Once undressed, the inmates were packed into gas chambers by **Sonderkommandos** (Special Squads).

The gassing was carried out by SS personnel who tipped the Zyklon B pellets into ducts in the ceiling or walls of the gas-chambers. Within about five minutes 2,000 corpses were all that remained in the larger chambers and 1,000 in the smaller ones.

The Sonderkommando would then move in, removing any gold dental fixtures, before loading the bodies on to metal trolleys for transport to the crematoria. There the bodies were pushed into the furnaces at enormous speed by the Jewish slaves. The Sonderkommandos were periodically exterminated and replaced with fresh inmates to minimize the possibility of rebellion.

Meantime, the possessions, clothes and hair of the victims were sorted, marked, packed for sending back to Germany in the same train that had brought them. To destroy the evidence, the huge amount of ashes produced daily was loaded on to trucks and spread in the marshes adjoining the camp, or used as fertilizer on an SS farm nearby.

Auschwitz was the greatest camp complex.

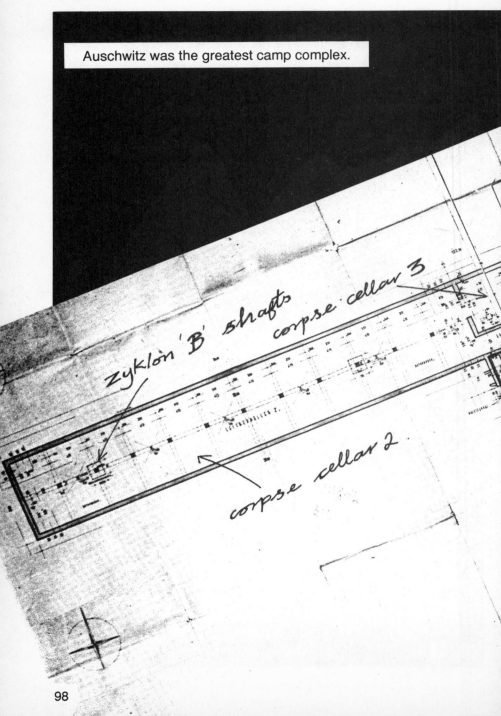

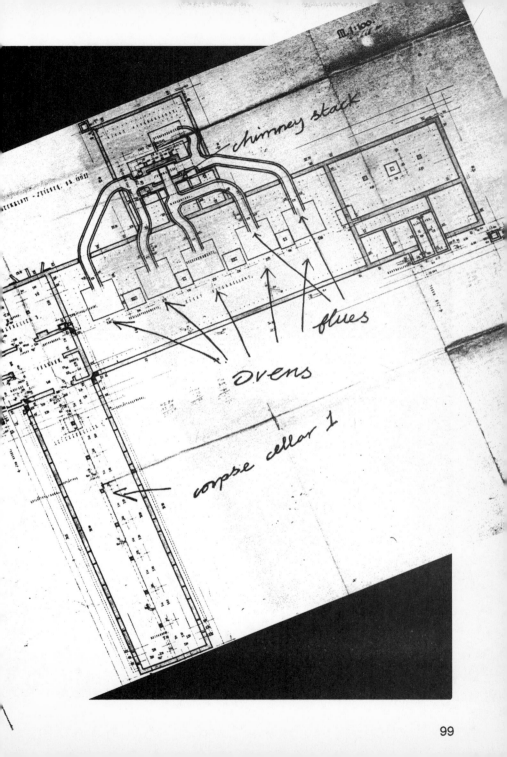

chimney stack

flues

Ovens

corpse cellar 1

99

In the summer of 1941, Rudolf Hoess (1900-47), a committed Nazi, was told in great secrecy by Himmler of Hitler's decision to destroy the Jewish people. He was commissioned to plan, build and operate a camp at Auschwitz (Oswiecim), an obscure but important railway junction in southern Poland.

AUSCHWITZ I

Auschwitz was made
up of three camps.

Auschwitz I: This housed
captured partisans, political
prisoners and POWs, mainly from
Poland and the USSR, homosexuals,
Jehovah's Witnesses and Jews. It was a
concentration and labour camp, rather than an
extermination one, although a large number of
Jews and others were killed there.

The whole Auschwitz complex was
administered from this camp. This included
co-ordinating the arrival of trains and
preparations for the reception of the deportees,
according to whether they were selected for
labour or for killing. Within the Auschwitz I
camp, there were plants belonging to Siemens,
DAW and Krupp, all producing armaments and
spare parts.

Auschwitz II: This was the purpose-built extermination centre at Birkenau, two miles from Auschwitz I. At least a million Jews died here.

In January 1942, 12,000 Russian POWs built over 200 wooden huts, 100 feet by 30 feet,each designed for 200 inmates but normally housing many times that number. The camp had no inner roads, and very few amenities of any kind, apart from some special "toilet huts", to which the inmates were marched once a day. Two minutes were allotted to the process. The number of inmates fluctuated between a few tens of thousands and over 120,000.

The Birkenau inmates were doomed. They were considered to be dead but temporarily reprieved by, for instance, congestion at the gas chambers. Unlike the inmates of Auschwitz I, they were not registered and tattooed with a number. There was no point in doing so. At one end of the camp, along a railway spur, were four gas chambers with their adjoining crematoria. The combined capacity of all four gas chambers was over 12,000 bodies a day. There were long periods during the war when the facility was working at full capacity, day and night, especially during the summer of 1944, when over 500,000 Hungarian Jews were gassed in less than two months.

Auschwitz III:

This was a huge plant
built by IG Farben, the giant
chemical concern, for the
manufacture - using the slave
labour of inmates, mainly Jews
- of synthetic rubber, synthetic fuel
and other chemicals of great strategic
importance to the Nazi war effort.
IG Farben made an investment of 700 million
Reichsmarks in the plant. Two coal mines
in the area, necessary for the production of
synthetic rubber (Buna), were taken over. Most of
the funds came from IG Farben, while the SS contributed
the predominantly Jewish slave labour.

Though the latest technology was used in building the plant, the work practices were the brutal ones of the concentration camp. Out of almost 40,000 inmates who worked there, over 25,000 died.

IG Farben was not the only concern to move to Auschwitz III to make use of the slave labour. Other companies included Krone-Presswerk, Graetz and Krupp.

The camp routine

Life in the camps was caught in a huge contradiction. On the one hand, there was the business of destruction. On the other, there was the desire to exploit the inmates to the utmost as a labour force.

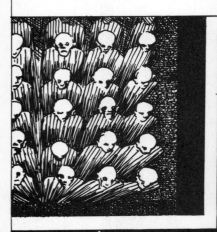

The camp commandants set up a system of internal administration which made the German political prisoners the ruling elite, with Slavs serving under them. Jews were permitted to serve only in the lower echelons of the internal bureaucracy.

A camp like Birkenau was divided into blocks, comprising a number of barracks, each housing a few 100 prisoners.

Certain inmates were given positions of power and were answerable to the Nazi authorities. Those overseeing the work details included the notorious Kapos (overseers) who enjoyed better conditions than the other inmates (including access to the camp brothel). The Block Clerks... inmates who provided the bureaucracy required for running the camp and separate blocks - also enjoyed certain privileges, such as separate sleeping-quarters and better food and clothes. These made their survival probable.

The Block Clerks were not only responsible for the roll-call of all inmates, but also for food distribution, maintenance of the huts and selections for the gas chambers.

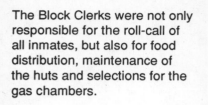

They were also responsible for corporal punishment administered in public in the presence of their German masters. The Germans also used a vast system of camp spies and collaborators, who, for a slice of bread, would give details of any attempts by the inmates to organize.

The combination of stratifiation on racial lines and a police-state machinery made resistance almost impossible.

The reality of daily life in the killing centres was one of graduated horror. The Jews in the work details subsisted on a diet of watery turnip soup in the morning, and bread that was largely sawdust in the evening. Many died each day as a result of starvation and maltreatment.

Unique features of the Holocaust

The Holocaust was the first modern genocide, totally dependent on modern technology and science, on the state bureaucracy and its immense ability to solve administrative and logistical problems, and on modern business and industrial techniques.

The whole process of mass production - from the early identification and isolation of the Jews to their final extermination - was perfected with the full co-operation and collusion of German industry.

Leading firms benefited enormously from the Final Solution at various stages - from the forced purchase of Jewish businesses to the labour of Jewish slaves in their advanced industrial plants, built in and around the death and concentration camps.

In September 1942, an agreement was reached between the RHSA and the Ministry of Justice. Under this agreement, "asocial elements" - broadly defined as Jews, Ukrainians, Russians, gypsies and Poles, but also Czech and German criminals - would no longer be the responsibility of the justice system, but would be handed to Himmler's RHSA organization for "Extermination through work" (**Vernichtung durch Arbeit**).

It is no accident, then, that the Auschwitz gate carried the slogan "Work makes one free" (**Arbeit Macht Frei**).

These conditions were due in part to a power struggle in the Nazi system. Himmler, the head of the SS and second only to Hitler, aimed to build an autonomous financial empire owned and run by the SS.

But Albert Speer (1905-81), the minister responsible for the war economy, saw this empire-building as detrimental to the war effort, from which it diverted materials, personnel and transport.

He therefore instructed Himmler that the camps had to be self-financing, dependent on the wealth stripped from the Jewish victims. There was never an official budget for the Final Solution.

The normal exploitation of labour, at the heart of all capitalist enterprise, was here free from any restraint, legal, social or moral.

The slaves had no rights to protect themselves and were literally worked to death. There were always others to replace them. The life expectancy of the Jewish slaves in IG Farben's synthetic rubber plant at Auschwitz was three months. The workers in the nearby coal-mines of IG Farben had a life expectancy of one month.

The Business of Death

The killing centres were organized to use every bit of the Jewish inmates - from the clothes they came in, their shoes, the gold teeth which had to be extracted by "specialist commandos", down to their hair which was packed and sent back to the Reich to serve mainly for the insulation of submarine hulls.

Thousands of Jewish slaves were employed in the collection, sorting out and despatch of the various items.

Important concepts in the design and operation of the death machine were:

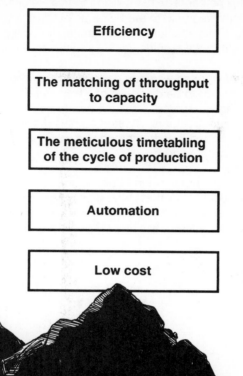

> **Efficiency**

> **The matching of throughput to capacity**

> **The meticulous timetabling of the cycle of production**

> **Automation**

> **Low cost**

An example:

The designers of the
cremation ovens at
Auschwitz had planned
to operate them with little or no fuel.
They would use instead the body fat
dripping from the corpses which would be
trapped in special trays. Because the fat content
of the bodies was so low as a result of starvation, the
system had to be abandoned as a total failure.
The firm that designed the crematoria was Tropf & Sons.
It patented the method in 1953.

The cost of a Jew's daily labour to the companies employing him or her was two Reichsmarks in 1941, rising to five Reichsmarks in 1944. The money was paid to the SS, thus helping to finance the killing process. This absolutely minimum labour cost provided the industrialists with huge surplus value of immense profits.

But many prisoners were so weak as a result of starvation that they died at work or had to be disposed of. This meant a constantly changing work force. Training had to be repeated, causing administrative problems. Written complaints to the SS camp commander argued that the companies were not getting their full value out of the workers.

There were arguments and memoranda in the best bureaucratic tradition over payments for workers who died on the premises, and hence did not deliver a full day's labour. Each side argued that the feeding of the workers was the responsibility of the other.

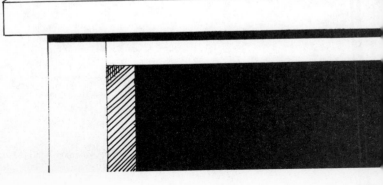

In most countries occupied by the Nazis, active armed resistance was limited to a small minority of the population. The same was true of the Jewish population.

Armed rebellion against Nazi forces was very difficult for the Jewish population, and in most cases pointless. Jews who had little access to arms and explosives, and usually no military training to fight against the Nazis effectively, had to be incorporated into an underground movement with wide support from the civilian population.

Where such conditions existed in Europe, Jews joined the partisans and fought bravely and effectively.

In Poland, however, Jews were often refused entry into the partisan groups, or even killed by the fiercely anti-Semitic Polish nationalist partisans.

The Jewish community in the ghettos was in general terrified of a strategy of resistance. It was seen as suicidal, given the overwhelming armed might of the Nazi forces. In a number of cases the Judenrat leader forced the Jewish underground leadership to surrender so as not to "endanger" the rest of the community.

In the Vilna ghetto, Yitzhak Wittenberg, who led a successful campaign mining German trains, surrendered under pressure from the Judenrat leader in order to "save the many". The SS had threatened to burn down the ghetto unless Wittenberg gave himself up.

He was killed. His group was forced to leave the ghetto for the forest, where they joined in partisan activities against the Nazi lines of communication.

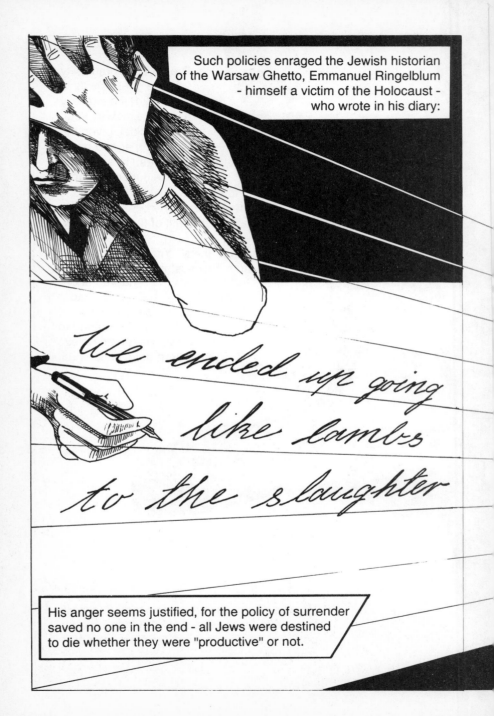

Such policies enraged the Jewish historian of the Warsaw Ghetto, Emmanuel Ringelblum - himself a victim of the Holocaust - who wrote in his diary:

We ended up going like lambs to the slaughter

His anger seems justified, for the policy of surrender saved no one in the end - all Jews were destined to die whether they were "productive" or not.

Those Jews who fought in hopeless circumstances did so for good reasons. They did not accept the argument that the instinct to survive had to be respected, because they saw that it preserved life only to end it in the gas chambers. They preferred to die fighting Nazism as an enemy of the human race.

Instances of rebellion tell an important story of human strength in the face of impossible adversity, of bravery born out of desperation, and devoid of heroic gestures.

The most prolonged armed resistance was put up by the inmates of the Warsaw Ghetto where the resistance organization, the Jewish Military Union, declared:

BROTHERS DON'T DIE IN SILENCE LET'S FIGHT

On 18 April the underground learned of a date set for the liquidation of the Ghetto. The 30,000 Jews still left took shelter in underground bunkers prepared in advance, and around 1,200 fighters, armed with two machine guns, 17 rifles, some useless pistols, and large numbers of homemade Molotov cocktails and grenades, prepared for a hopeless battle.

On Passover morning 19 April, 1943, a 3,200 strong SS brigade, equipped with heavy machine guns, howitzers, light artillery and armoured vehicles, moved into the Ghetto.

They came under fire from all sides, suffered losses in dead and wounded and retreated hastily.

After their losses on the first day, the SS used artillery to reduce the ghetto to rubble. The ruins were then swept by machine-gun fire and set alight with flame throwers. From across the ghetto boundaries, the Polish inhabitants watched the destruction, day after day, and saw people shot while trying to escape from the flames.

OUR DEATHS SHALL NOT BE MEANINGLESS

The Jews were not fighting for their lives; they were fighting so that their deaths would not be meaningless.

The rebellion lasted four weeks. When the ghetto was totally destroyed by shelling and mortar fire, the SS moved in, going from cellar to cellar and gassing the trapped Jews. Several thousand Jews were killed in this way; 30,000 were captured. The majority were immediately sent to the extermination camp at Treblinka. The last survivors were hunted down in the sewer system by sniffer dogs. All that remained of the ghetto was an open wound in the body of the capital, an area of destruction and pestilence. It was an exemplary and terrible punishment - a warning to others.

The Warsaw rising, and the reversal of the sterotype of the "meek and cowardly Jews", was of great importance to resistance fighters elsewhere. The battle for Warsaw also became crucial for the Nazi authorities, although it had no military rationale. The rebellion had to be squashed before other groups, in Poland and elsewhere, would start considering resistance to be a viable option. They were right in their fears. The Jewish Ghetto Rising was put down, but it inspired the equally tragic Polish Warsaw Rising of 1944.

The Treblinka Rebellion

In the summer of 1943, the Red Army was advancing towardsTreblinka, in eastern Poland. The SS started to open the mass graves in which hundreds of thousands of murdered Jews were buried and, with a huge mechanical digger, piled the bodies on great pyres which burned day and night.

The Jewish Sonderkommando, who numbered about 700 prisoners, understood that this was an attempt to destroy the evidence before the Red Army arrived.

127

The prisoners had
long been planning a revolt.
The chance to carry it out
came on 2 August 1943.

The key to the armoury had
been copied by a prisoner.
The plotters were thus able
to take out and conceal a
number of rifles and hand
grenades.

That afternoon,
the disinfection team
sprayed the camp structures as usual,
but used petrol in the sprayers. Most of the camp,
built of wood, caught fire within minutes. As the SS
and the Ukrainian guards tried to regain control, the
rebels fought their way out of the camp.

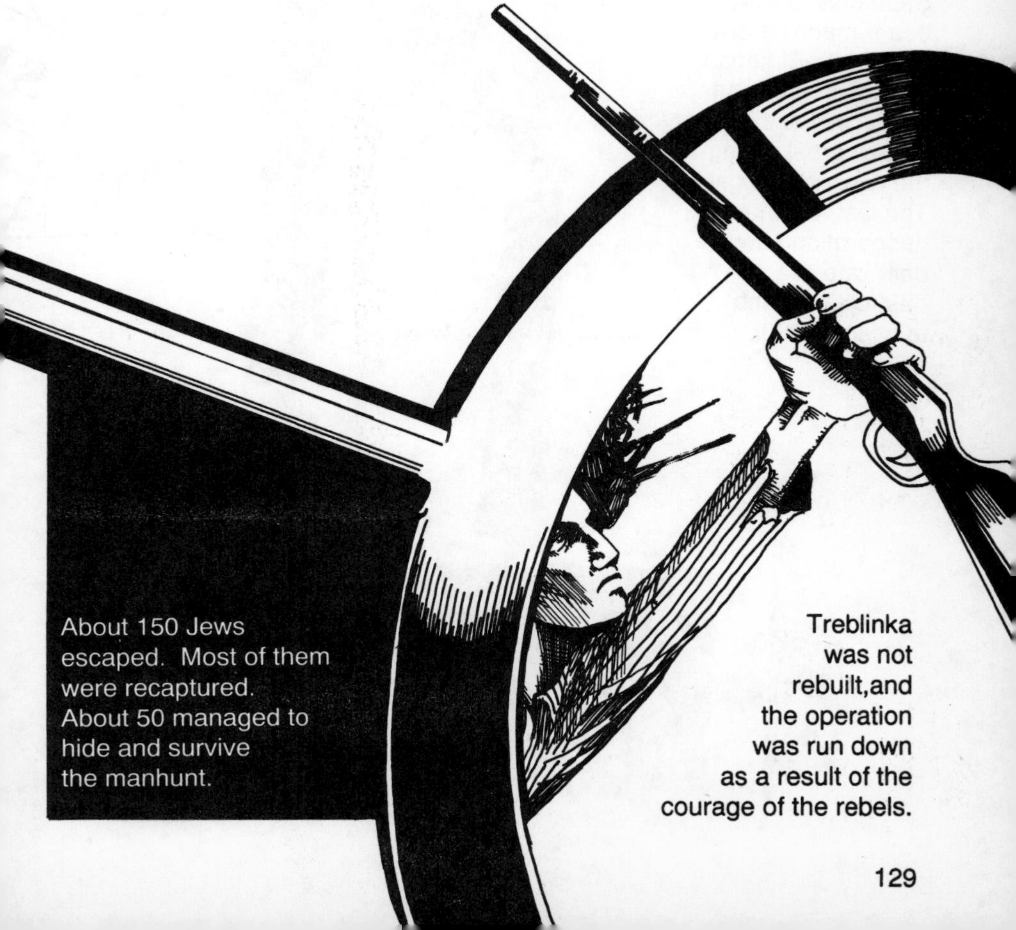

About 150 Jews
escaped. Most of them
were recaptured.
About 50 managed to
hide and survive
the manhunt.

Treblinka
was not
rebuilt,and
the operation
was run down
as a result of the
courage of the rebels.

MAY 1944

M	T	W	T
4	5	6	
11	12	13	
18	19	20	
25	26		

JUNE 1944

M	T	W	T	F			S	S
		1	2					
6	7	8						
13	14	15	16					
20	21	22	23					
27	28	29	30					

JULY 1944

M	T	W	T		
1	2				
8	9	10	11	18	19
15	16	17		25	2
22	23	24			
29	30	3			

AUG

M	T	W
6		
13	14	
20	21	
27	28	2

S

Between May and September 1944, the death-machine of Auschwitz-Birkenau destroyed almost a million Jews, the largest group being the Jews of Hungary. The last few months of operation saw the daily rate of destruction climb to over 10,000.

With the Red Army close at hand, the order was given to destroy the gas chambers and crematoria and remove all evidence. The inmates were aware that the camp was about to be wound up and knew that, as witnesses, their days were numbered. The camp underground ordered a rebellion on 7 October 1944.

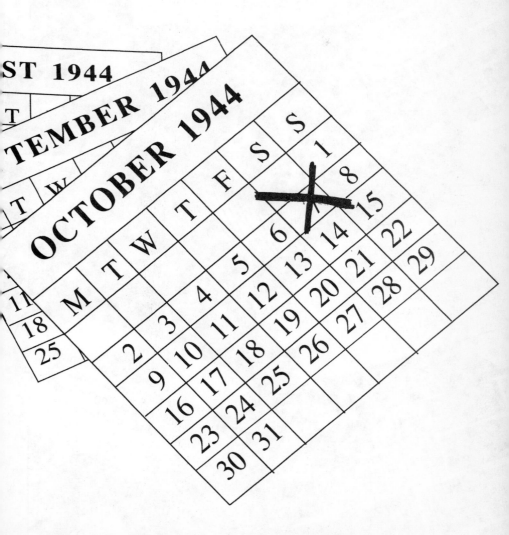

At the last moment
the uprising was called off.
But the most vulnerable group,
the Jewish Sonderkommando,
did not accept the decision.

Using explosives
smuggled in by four
Jewish women
factory-workers,
they blew up
the crematoria...

and killed...
a number of SS personnel
with the long hooks
used for pulling bodies
out of the gas chambers.

The few hundred members of the Kommando
were hunted down and shot.

The four women were hanged.

The SS themselves completed the destruction of
the installation, blowing up the crematoria,
removing all evidence of the real function
of the camp.

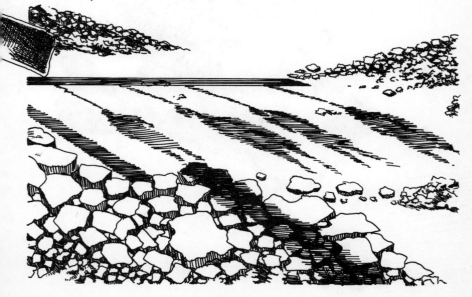

The Jews of Hungary

Before the war, there were over 700,000 Jews in Hungary. During the war, refugees from other countries swelled that number to 800,000.

The Jews of Hungary presented the Nazis with a problem. They were a fully integrated community. Although Hungary was a wartime ally of Nazi Germany, and had a fully-fledged fascist government, there were no ghettos and the Jews were not segregated in any way.

It is true that in 1938 Hungary had begun the "legal definition" of Jews that would oust them from the financial life of the country.

The Jews' special position can be explained by the fact that they were predominantly middle class and could not easily be dislodged without damaging the fabric of Hungarian society.
As late as mid-1944, the Manfred-Weiss concern, owned by the Jewish millionaire Baron Weiss, was the largest munitions factory serving the Third Reich.

The Hungarian nationalists were reluctant to surrender their Jews to the Nazis or carry out mass deportations.

Though by March 1944 the Nazi war effort was collapsing, Hitler was so obsessed by the need to exterminate this large, intact Jewish community that he summoned Admiral Miklos Horthy de Nagybanya (1868-1957) the Hungarian head of state.

YOU MUST CHOOSE BETWEEN GERMAN OCCUPATION OF HUNGARY OR THE IMMEDIATE APPOINTMENT OF A GOVERNMENT APPROVED BY ME!

Hitler also gave an ultimatum: the "solution" of the Jewish question in Hungary was long overdue and must start immediately.

Horthy obediently appointed a fascist prime minister. A German plenipotentiary - in effect, a German governor of Hungary - was installed in Budapest, bringing with him Eichmann and his staff and their bureaucracy of destruction.

Meanwhile, the Hungarian administration started legislating at enormous speed.

Jews are barred from occupations

(This did not include medicine, as a quarter of Hungary's qualified medical personnel were Jews.)

Jews are required to wear the Jewish Star of David

Jews are prohibited from travelling without a police special permit and are to be placed under curfew.

Jewish stores and businesses are to be confiscated

Jewish stores and businesses were forced through the same machinery of dispossession and confiscation as had been developed in Germany. Within a few days, all Jewish stores were closed - over a third of all businesses in Hungary. All Jewish bank accounts were frozen.

The Jewish population was left with no means of survival.

Eichmann was faced by an operation that was more difficult than elsewhere. In Poland he had the support of the German governors of the occupied territories, of the German army and the Einsatzgruppen. His staff was small for the size of the task. Time was pressing. The Red Army was advancing rapidly, the Second Front was imminent in the West.

His first step was to meet the Jewish Council of Budapest and demand a full report on the community's property. Then he ordered the immediate setting up of a Judenrat which would be the only body recognized by the SS and responsible for carrying out their orders. This was the same machine for collaboration as had worked in the Polish ghettos. Eichmann promised that no harm would come to those who co-operated fully.

I REGRET THE CONTROL MEASURES WHICH ARE TEMPORARY AND GUARANTEE THE SAFETY OF THE HUNGARIAN JEWS.

Eichmann thus achieved an enormous feat - the Judenräte was committed to collaborating with him in carrying out his measures, believing this to be the safer option.

But while the Polish Judenräte, especially in the early days, could be forgiven for such naivety, the case was very different in Hungary.

your fate is far from sealed

knowledge about us has got out to the allies

the Nazis are in a desperate military and political situation

Very soon the Jews of the outlying regions of Hungary were being concentrated near mainline stations. This operation was the swiftest Europe had yet seen. From these concentration camps, the Jews were deported to Poland at a death rate of some 12,000 a day.

At all times, the Judenrat knew what was happening to the deported Jews. Eichmann spelt it out to them. The leaders decided to keep this knowledge to themselves. They went so far as to fabricate postcards from a nonexistent work camp with optimistic reports about food and conditions, in order to entice those left behind to join them.

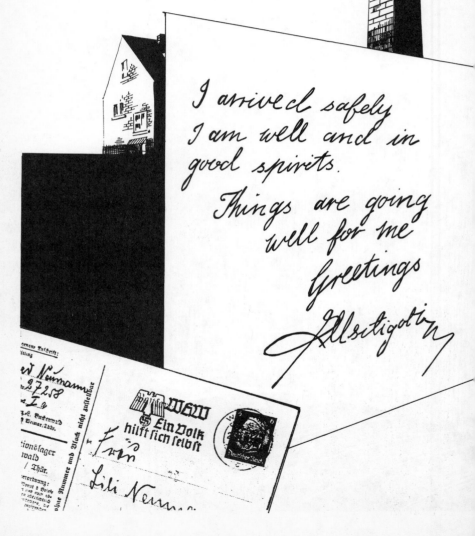

I arrived safely
I am well and in
good spirits.

Things are going
well for me

Greetings

The co-operation of the Hungarian police, the Judenrat, the civil service and the population generally helped to make the Hungarian deportations almost peaceful. The Jews trusted their leadership, preferring in many instances to volunteer for earlier deportation so as to be together with friends or family.

At times Auschwitz-Birkenau could not cope with the transports.
Because of the limited capacity of the furnaces, corpses had to be
burned in open trenches. Speed was essential because the Red Army
was moving towards the camp. In little over two months, the bulk of the
Jews of Hungary had been killed.

An international effort was started by a number of
individuals and European states to halt the
deportations.

Tens of thousands of Jews were
saved by the Swedish diplomat,
Raoul Wallenberg, who supplied
them with false documents,
communal passports and safe
houses in Budapest which he
declared to be extraterritorial.

The *Prominenten* Deal

Seeing that the end of the Third Reich was inevitable, some SS operatives calculated that, if they saved some Jewish lives, this might stand them in good stead later.

There were two such initiatives. In one, the SS - partly to reward the Hungarian Judenrat - agreed to free 1,600 Jews, the so-called **"Prominenten"**, who were mainly council members and their kin, and send them to safety in Switzerland. This was only to take place after the completion of the deportations. The "Prominenten" thus became the hostages for this process. They were indeed released and sent to Switzerland towards the end of the war.

Eichmann's Deal

The other initiative, which had Himmler's approval, was proposed by Eichmann himself to Joel Brand, a prominent Budapest Jew.   The offer was to spare a million Jews. Their lives were to be paid for in kind - with military trucks to be used only on the Russian front. The price was one truck for every 100 Jews. Brand had three weeks to fix the deal.

Brand travelled to Turkey and the Middle East hoping to contact a member of the Jewish Agency, the representative of Zionism in Palestine, who would in turn approach the British.

But Brand was
arrested by British agents
and kept a prisoner.

Meanwhile, the Jews died
at the rate of 10,000 per day.

The Jewish Agency and the British authorities were at one in their refusal to consider Eichmann's offer. The Jewish Agency did not see its priority to be saving Jews in Europe, but rather that of populating Palestine with highly motivated Zionist settlers.

Nor were the British eager to receive the refugees from Hungary.
While Brand was in British hands, a high British official said to him...

Moreover, the British and Americans were alarmed that the deal would be seen by the Russians, who were already rightly complaining that they were bearing the brunt of the war on land, as a negotiation with the enemy clearly to their disadvantage.
No doubt the Nazis were aware of the dilemma they presented to the Allies and of its potential to cause a rift.

WHAT AM I TO DO WITH A MILLION JEWS? WHERE SHALL I PUT THEM?

One of the persons
involved in both initiatives
was Rudolf Kazstner,
associate president of the
Zionist Organization in
Hungary.

He was protected by the
Nazis until the end of the
war, travelling with a
high-ranking officer of the
SS, in his attempt to
negotiate in Switzerland.

Kazstner later gave
evidence that saved this
officer from the Nuremberg
War Crime Trials.

After the war, Kazstner was himself tried *in absentia* by a people's court of Budapest Jews. He was found guilty of collaboration with the Nazis and of furthering their policy of destroying the Hungarian Jews. He was sentenced to death. Having emigrated to Israel, he held a junior ministerial post for a number of years, before being assassinated by two young survivors from Hungary who considered themselves to be meting out the justice of history.

It has been argued that the Allies had no reliable information about the Final Solution until the war was over. They could not therefore be blamed for not intervening to stop the process - by bombing the death camps, for instance.

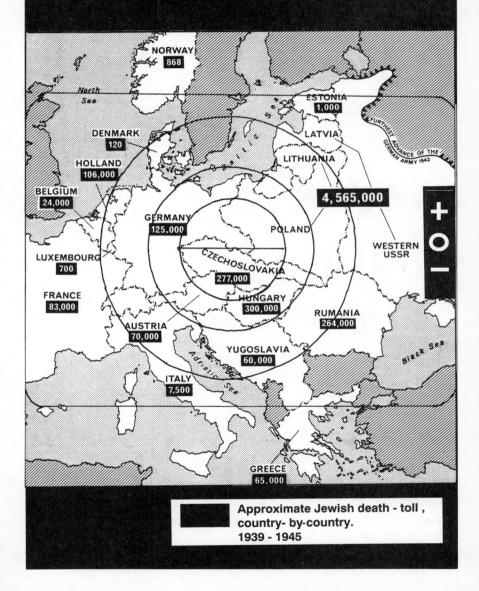

NORWAY
868

North Sea

ESTONIA
1,000

LATVIA

DENMARK
120

LITHUANIA

FURTHEST ADVANCE OF THE GERMAN ARMY 1942

HOLLAND
106,000

BELGIUM
24,000

GERMANY
125,000

POLAND

4,565,000

WESTERN USSR

LUXEMBOURG
700

CZECHOSLOVAKIA
277,000

FRANCE
83,000

HUNGARY
300,000

RUMANIA
264,000

AUSTRIA
70,000

YUGOSLAVIA
60,000

Adriatic Sea

Black Sea

ITALY
7,500

GREECE
65,000

Approximate Jewish death - toll , country- by-country. 1939 - 1945

But numerous reports were received by the Allies from December 1941 on. These included maps showing the organization of the killing centres. The most important was delivered in 1942 by two Czech Jews who managed to escape from Auschwitz, bringing with them extremely accurate information about the camps and the numbers killed since 1941. Both had worked as registrars in the camp bureaucracy, and so had had access to the most secret of all Nazi documents.

Their report led to demands by prominent Jews, especially in the USA, for the bombing of the camps and their communication links in order to disable or destroy the death machine.

The Allies' scepticism about the truth of these reports reflected basic anti-Semitism. The BBC did not mention the crucial part of Foreign Secretary Anthony Eden's report to the Commons in December 1942.

GERMANY IS CARRYING INTO EFFECT HITLER'S OFTEN REPEATED INTENTION TO EXTERMINATE THE JEWISH PEOPLE IN EUROPE.

A curious logic led the BBC management to argue that mention of the plight of the Jews might inflame anti-Jewish feelings in Britain. The BBC was to limit itself to reporting "the facts...of Jewish persecution", but there was to be no "propaganda".

In 1944, an under-secretary at the Foreign Office dismissed stories of the gas chambers as "atrocity stories for which we have no evidence". Another official dismissed the reports because they came from "Jewish sources".

PERSONALLY I HAVE NEVER REALLY UNDERSTOOD THE ADVANTAGE OF THE GAS CHAMBERS OVER THE SIMPLER MACHINE GUN OR THE EQUALLY SIMPLE STARVATION METHOD

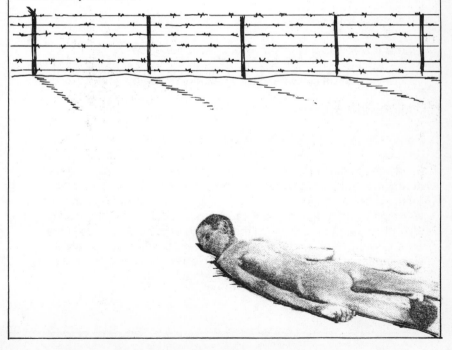

In spite of the demands from prominent Jews, and the knowledge on which they were based, there were long delays in getting aerial photographs, and long discussions about whether or not to bomb the camps. The operation, it was argued, would divert considerable air support essential for the success of Allied operations. So Auschwitz was not bombed until August 1944 by Allied planes from Italy. By then, the Allies had full aerial photographs of the camps, but curiously analysis did not identify the chimneys of the crematoria, which were clearly visible on an aerial photograph taken that month. The death camp was not the target, but rather the industrial synthetic rubber plant in Auschwitz III.

Renewed requests for bombing the gas chambers met with further procrastination. In the end, the decision was taken at the highest levels not to carry out the bombings. The operation would endanger the lives of too many aircrews.

The Revisionist Historians

Academics have played an important and conscious part in supporting, elaborating and propagating the ideology of the Third Reich. A school of historians and polemicists has sprung up, which for political reasons is bent on denying the truth of the story of the Holocaust. Present day revisionists continue this tradition. They are the academic equivalent of the neo-Nazi thugs.

One of the most important early revisionists was Paul Rassinier (1906-1967), a French school teacher and reformist socialist, who was himself an inmate of Buchenwald and worked in a labour camp. He cast doubt on accounts of the extermination camps, exploiting the kinds of contradictions which are common when witnesses depend on memory. The apparent reasonableness of his argument concealed his deeply reactionary and bitterly anti-humanist views.

He also developed a complicated "numbers game" to prove that there could not have been 6 million deaths. Here he relied on contradictions which derive from different ways of breaking down the available statistics.

His conclusions were:

- there never was a Nazi policy of Jewish genocide

- there was no officially sanctioned extermination by gas

- there were not 6 million Jewish victims

He admits that Hitler's policy against the Jews was "an unquestionable attack on human rights", and that deaths were "an unfortunate coincidence", usually occurring during transit. But never at any moment, he asserted, did the responsible authorities of the Third Reich intend to order the extinction of the Jews. Atrocities were the work of one or two insane persons in the SS. If gassing took place, it had a parallel in the gassing of criminals in the United States, where it was a perfectly legal form of execution. But there was, in his view, nothing to prove conclusively that any of the unfit or those so designated were sent to the death chambers.

His arguments have been taken up by publications and writers on the neo-Fascist right in Europe, including Britain, and in the United States where one of the most vocal revisionists designs systems for the death chambers in state prisons.

In spite of the fact that the bulk of the Jews of Occupied Europe were shipped by train to the East and never returned -
in spite of the film shot by the Nazi authorities of transports arriving at the camps -
in spite of the photographs of men, women and children lined up awaiting death by shooting or in the death chambers -
in spite of such Nazi documentation as the technical drawings for the crematoria -
in spite of the installations still remaining at sites like Auschwitz -
in spite of the evidence of survivors -
the revisionists still brazenly proclaim that Nazism has been falsely accused.

Their publications are yet another attempt to resurrect Fascism, to find in "the Jew" (and in other minorities) that "Other" on which Fascism has traditionally discharged its irrational hates and fears.

Unfortunately, the fabrications of the "revisionists" have fallen on fertile ground in a Europe where the old lies of anti-Semitic propaganda and old forgeries are once again being circulated, and indeed were never wholly eradicated.

PAUL RASSINIER

No Evidence?

A Poet in Auschwitz

In 1967, the Austrian poet Erich Fried, a Viennese Jew who had managed to emigrate to Britain, visited Auschwitz. He had some idea what to expect, but some things surprised him. The hair shorn from the victims was not a great mound, but flat. He had expected the mountain of shoes, but the huge heap of spectacles surprised him as did the pile of artificial arms and legs. But, he wrote, "even more surprising was the mountain of children's toys."

"Somewhat helplessly I looked at the pile of toys partly damaged, partly well-preserved. Suddenly I saw Moritz. Moritz was about ten inches high, red-haired, with a green jacket and green trousers. He was on wheels, so that when he was pulled along on a string he alternately bent forward and leant back. At the same time he also swung his arms and legs... It was a reunion. Moritz had been my own doll, broken when I was four years old, but now completely undamaged. As a child I had of course never considered Moritz as mass produced but I cannot ever remember seeing a second Moritz in a toy shop or in the park where I played. Only in Auschwitz, more than forty years after my doll was broken, did I see its double."

At another point he saw what looked like his grandmother's spice box.

"Like my mobile doll, Moritz, our spice box had at sometime or other, when my grandfather bought it, been a mass-produced object... Many people, old ones from my grandmother's generation... were deported to the East 'for resettlement', as it was called.....and full of hope they took a few of their smaller household objects with them.

So the spice -box with the fancy blue writing came to Auschwitz. Not with my grandmother. She had been gassed, it is true, at the age of seventy-six; but she had already arrived at her penultimate station, Theresienstadt, (the concentration camp for older Jews), without heavy luggage, because she was blind and frail and could not carry much."

(From *My Doll in Auschwitz*, in **Children and Fools** by Erich Fried, translated by Martin Chalmers, Serpent's Tail, London 1992)

The Aftermath

The Nuremberg and other war trials,
Anti-Semitism and the Zionist view
of the Holocaust.

1. War Crimes and Trials

In 1945, an International Military Tribunal was set up to prosecute
Nazi war criminals. It was to deal with Crimes against Peace,
War Crimes and Crimes against Humanity. The Holocaust came
under the last heading.

Meeting at Nuremberg, the Tribunal tried a group of leading
Nazis, which included Heydrich's successor as chief of the Reich
Main Security Office, and Hans Frank, the Governor-General of
occupied Poland. Twelve were sentenced to death, three (who
included Hitler's deputy, Rudolf Hess) were imprisoned for life,
others got shorter prison sentences and four were discharged.
Hitler, Himmler and Goering had all committed suicide, the latter
with the connivance of an American prison guard.

There were other subsequent trials, and some of the main culprits
were condemned to death. These included men like Oswald
Pohl, who ran the SS slave labour programme, and Rudolf Franz
Hoess who set up Auschwitz. But it was clear from the beginning
that the pursuit and punishment of war criminals - particularly in
the British zone of occupation - had a low priority. The process
was allowed to drag on, handicapped by ignorance, by
bureaucratic confusion, by political reluctance, by anti-Semitism
(some of the investigators and prosecutors, particularly in the
American Zone, were Jewish), and by professional and class
solidarity with certain criminals like Field Marshals Gerd von
Rundstedt and Fritz Erich von Manstein, the latter having issued
a directive to army commanders saying that "the soldier must
appreciate the need for the harsh punishment of Jewry, the
spiritual bearer of the Bolshevik terror". A public subscription was
opened in Britain for the defence costs of von Manstein, described
as "an aged German general" who had only murdered Russians
and Poles. Churchill was one of the first to contribute; £2,000
was raised - a large sum in those days. The officers of the British
War Crimes Group, with few exceptions, resigned rather than help
with the prosecution of von Rundstedt. Indeed, they gave a
dinner in the Marshal's honour. "A person of his calibre deserved
the honour, and he was very touched," said the officer who
organized the occasion.

The Cold War played its part in sowing suspicion between the Russians and the Western Allies. In the United States, a Congressman had accused the war crime investigators in the American Zone of being "a racial minority" who were "hanging German soldiers and trying German businessmen in the name of the United States". In 1949, Senator Joseph McCarthy attacked foreign-born Jews who were "abusing the procedures of American justice", and campaigned for the death sentence of a Buchenwald guard officer to be commuted. In 1951, that officer - Hans Schmidt - became the last war criminal to be executed by the Allies.

Of the thousands involved in war crimes and the Holocaust, only a fraction were tracked down and brought to justice. Many that were received relatively light sentences. Typical is the case of Alfried Krupp, the head of the great steel firm. He had made extensive use of slave labour and was sentenced in 1948 to 12 years and loss of all his possessions. In 1951, he was released and subsequently reinstated. Dr Abbs, the banker who had funded IG Farben and was on its board, but denied any knowledge of Auschwitz III, lost his 45 directorships - but was never tried. Instead, to his own surprise and relief, he was invited by the British to rebuild the German banking system. Otto Ambros, who chose the site at Auschwitz for IG Farben, was given eight years. After his release, he emigrated to the United States where he became adviser to an American company and consultant to the Department of Energy under the Reagan administration. The company did not feel there was anything wrong in employing him, "years after whatever he did".

In 1960, Adolf Eichmann was spirited out of hiding in Argentina by Mossad, the Israeli secret service, and a show trial was held in Jerusalem. Lasting over a year, it transfixed Israelis and representatives of the world media. Eichmann was executed in 1962. Unfortunately, an opportunity to understand the Holocaust was not just missed - it was carefully avoided.Instead, a process of dehumanization took place, which explained little and covered up a great deal. The single voice of reason to come out of Jerusalem, that of Hannah Arendt, the distinguished American scholar who coined the term "banality of evil" which Eichmann embodied for her, was derided. Similarly, the analysis of the Holocaust by the historian Raul Hilberg has been dismissed because it concentrates on functionalist arguments - that is to say, those which consider that the tragedy was determined by a number of political and other factors, rather than relying on the emotionalism of irrational, ahistorical anti-Semitism.

As a force for the creation of national coherence in Israel, the Eichmann trial served its purpose well. A semi-fictitious explanation of the historical events had its effect. In the Israel of the 1960s, the need for such a unifying force was paramount.

The more recent extradition from the United States and subsequent trial of Ivan Demjaniuk, alias "Ivan the Terrible" of Treblinka, was an attempt at a replay of the Eichmann trial. The fact that the accused is not "Ivan the Terrible" himself, but only "Ivan-the-not-so-Terrible", a Ukrainian guard serving in the camps, like so many tens of thousands of others who were never tried, is neither here nor there. Once again the trial served its purpose. Show trials never fail, as the experience shows in many cases - in Nazi Germany, in Stalin's Soviet Union or in the American "witchhunt trials" under McCarthyism. These show trials are an exploitation of the Holocaust which is difficult to justify.

2. The Endurance of Anti-Semitism

The lack of Jews to hate in the newly **Judenrein** countries of eastern Europe did not stop anti-Semitism in those countries after the war. Even while the postwar Soviet system was at its peak, periodic displays of both officially sanctioned and freelance anti-Semitism were never far away. In Poland, the Jews - of which there were precious few - were hated with ferocity, owing to the central roles many played in the Communist party and state machineries. The Polish Jews reached their positions in the party after many years of fighting fascism and of personal suffering. But their new, powerful and protected status did nothing to endear them to a population brought up on its own brand of racism, which had been fortified by collaboration in Nazi practices during the war. A particularly disturbing example is that in the National Museum at Auschwitz, there is no mention that most of the 4 million "Poles" killed by the Nazis were Jewish. In the killing-field of a million Jews, Birkenau, there is no attempt to record or describe what happened there.The old Nazi maxim, that "behind the Bolsheviks are the Jews", acquired a new life in the postwar countries of east Europe and anti-Semitism still persists there after the collapse of Communism.

In countries where the Final Solution had wiped out the Jews, it did not wipe out anti-Semitism. In Poland, within nine months of the end of the war, over 1,000 Jews were murdered in a series of pogroms - the most famous being at Kielce, where more than 100 survivors of Auschwitz were massacred, with the Communist government seemingly powerless to stem the tide. The Third Reich had gone, but the terror of the Final Solution was still lurking in Europe. The hundreds of thousands of Jewish refugees who had survived had to be found somewhere to go. The West was unwilling to pay the price of resettling them, and therefore agreed to a colonial solution in Palestine.

3. The Zionist View of the Holocaust

It is doubtful whether the UN would have decided in 1947 to divide Palestine into two states, an Arab and a Jewish state, but for the fact that a safe haven was not found anywhere for the survivors. The creation of a Jewish state geographically remote from "the West" was a way of soaking up the guilt.

The state of Israel itself took a relatively small number of refugees. But this did not stop the Israeli government from negotiating with the new West German *Bundesrepublik* as sole self-appointed agent not only of the survivors living in Israel, but also of all the dead Jews who left no heirs. As a result, the Germans agreed a wide-ranging programme of reparations to be paid directly to the Israeli government, rather than to the survivors. The Israelis were then responsible for paying individuals their personal reparations on behalf of the *Bundesrepublik*. Like most agents, they paid only a small proportion to the individuals concerned. The "Israeli" payments were less than a third of the equivalent paid directly by the *Bundesrepublik* to individual non-Israeli survivors. This was reminiscent of the Transfer Agreement (Ha'avara) negotiated between the prewar Nazi government and the Zionist Federation. In both cases, governments and national institutions benefited from the personal misery of Jewish refugees.

Nor was the *Bundesrepublik* being purely charitable. It used the reparations programme to export German technology to Israel – most of the programme being paid in kind. The power stations, irrigation projects, factories and industrial plant and, later, armaments, imported from Germany played an important part in the rebuilding of the German economy. But even in material terms, the *Bundesrepublik* did not pay back more than a small part of the property of the murdered millions.

Recently, hard evidence has been found for scandalous treatment of the Jewish victims and survivors by many European companies and governments, not just those of Nazi Germany. A huge Italian insurance company, the Swiss banking system, many commercial companies which have grown thanks to Jewish and Russian POW slave labour, even the Amsterdam municipality – all are blamed for taking over the property of dead Jews. In many of the negotiating bodies which have appeared in the last decade, what was established was the apparently exclusive right of the Israeli state and its agencies to speak for the dead Jews. This not only put Israel above and beyond normal international standards of behaviour; it also meant that the guilt complex of the West could be further exploited. Through the postwar decades, thanks largely to the support of most US administrations, Israel has secured its place at the heart of Western politics, in financial, political, military and diplomatic terms. This position has not been shaken, despite the suffering caused in the Middle East by this policy. Thus, the Israeli military occupation of a number of Arab countries, and all of the Palestinian territories, has not led to any concerted efforts against Israel in the fashion that was used against Apartheid, Libya, Iraq or, more recently, Serbia or Indonesia.

This has meant that the West has gradually succumbed to more and more racist measures applied by Israel to the Palestinians, who are their own "Other". While it is totally unfair and inaccurate to compare the Israeli occupation of Eastern Palestine since 1967 to the Nazi occupation of Europe, there are undoubtedly similarities between the Israeli occupation and some of the worst, most racist occupations elsewhere. Those similarities have now become part of the structure of Israeli society. This has produced ideas, practices and policies that resemble those found in Germany in the 1930s.

In the aftermath of the Holocaust, there has, in general, been a disturbing lack of rational debate of its deep reasons and enabling factors. Nowhere is this truer than in Israel.

Israel has adopted the role of "Speaker for the Jewish Dead" and custodian of the Holocaust as a perfect ideological justification for its less-than-benign policies and actions in the Middle East. By so doing, Israel has made criticism of its actions almost impossible. It is automatically described as "anti-Semitic" or "Nazi". In the case of Jewish criticism, the critical voice is termed a "self-hating" Jew. The state-controlled Holocaust institutions – many of them well-financed – have not been merely academic, historical or commemorative organizations, but a crucial mainstay of the ideological and political struggle for control of an agenda which includes the occupation of Palestine – and control of the debate that surrounds it.

The dominance of Yad Vashem in Jerusalem, for many years the main institute in the field of Holocaust research, has skewed the debate exclusively towards those topics and attitudes which have been thought beneficial to the Israeli official perspective. This has affected the received image of the Holocaust, not only in Israel but elsewhere.

One important tendency in official discussion of the Holocaust has been to put to one side any explanation which is not based on **intentionalism** – that is to say, the view that the Holocaust was planned from the beginning by the Nazis – or which does not see anti-Semitism as the exclusive motivating force behind it. The Nazis are seen in isolation, and the Allies and their less-than-glorious role are left out of the debate altogether. Any argument which would draw similarities with genocides elsewhere has been rejected out of hand. There has been great resistance to any explanations based on historical and social analysis. The name "Holocaust" is protected ferociously against "improper use" – for instance, when applied to any case of genocide such as the Turkish massacre of the Armenians in 1915.

Only in the last couple of decades, through the emergence of independent research centres elsewhere, has this view been gradually undermined and a better understanding evolved of the whole process leading to the Final Solution. Ironically, such widespread research has also helped popular representations of the Holocaust, such as the film *Schindler's List* (which was seen by millions everywhere), and has helped to sensitize many to the questions raised by the Holocaust. It is apt that the proceeds from this film are used to support Holocaust research at a number of centres internationally. The many museums and research institutions may help to spread an open and hybrid understanding of this period and its terrifying lessons.

The Inversion of Roles – Victim has become Executioner

Since 1948, the Jews in Israel (and indirectly through them, Jews elsewhere) have found themselves in an unusual situation, that of being the dispossessor, the stronger party, militarily and politically. While in Europe they suffered the total annihilation of the dispossessed, in Palestine they were the Europeans faced with a Third World "native" population. In that new situation, which Jews have not faced for millennia, the Jews in Palestine acted like typical colonists, with one exception – instead of a policy of exploitation of the locals, they adopted quite early a policy of expulsion, of transferring the locals to neighbouring countries. This was not just an expedient result of the 1948 war – it was already laid down as an operating principle of Zionism in Theodor Herzl's book **Judenstaat** (1895).

Probably as a result of the experiences of the 1930s and the Holocaust years, ideas of population "transfer", based on extreme racism, were popular enough to be represented at parliamentary level and to form a viable option for many Israelis, despite the real difficulties of putting such ideas into practice. As the railways are not quite as developed in Israel as in Europe, this "solution to the Palestinian problem" – termed the "lorry solution" by General Rechavam Ze'evi (known as "Gandhi"), a right-wing Israeli Member of Parliament – supplies the mainstay of at least one party on the Israeli right. Following the Oslo Agreement, and the withdrawals from Palestinian territory which were part of this agreement, the Israeli Premier who signed the agreement was murdered by a religious right-wing fanatic, who calculated that his death would stop the peace process. In the event, this calculation was right. Since Rabin's death in 1995, hardly any moves towards normalization have taken place. The religious right in Israel, basing itself on racist and supremacist tenets, is refusing to allow any human or national rights to the Palestinian Arabs. There could be no further departure from the liberal traditions of Judaism, especially against the background of Holocaust history.

Before 1948, Zionism was not in a position to apply this policy, but the war opened new options which led, time and again, to military occupation of its neighbours' territories, beginning in 1967. Israel has justified this behaviour by harking back to the horrors of the Holocaust, and on the whole this has been enough to silence opposition to its aggressive policies and acts. However, there is a substantial way in which those acts of aggression are indeed related to the Holocaust through a complex psycho-social dynamic – that of the identification of victim with executioner.

This dynamic may have been partially responsible for the exact manner of Israeli actions against the "natives", and the choices adopted. Both in the Occupied Territories of the West Bank and in southern Lebanon, which Israel has occupied since 1982, the thinking and actions are influenced by the methodology of occupation which enslaved Europe, and especially its Jews. Every act of resistance by the population, whether through non-violent direct action or through guerrilla acts, is seen as a total attack on the occupation authorities, and justifies communal punishment on a massive scale, making the Biblical "eye for an eye" look extremely humane. During July 1993, Israel reacted to the death of seven of its soldiers at the hands of local Muslim guerrillas in the occupied southern Lebanon "Security Zone" by launching their largest attack on civilians. Nearly half-a-million Lebanese have left their homes, fleeing north, driven away by the Israelis. These civilians were undisputably non-combatants, but they formed the pressure lever in a move designed to make that country "uninhabitable", according to Premier Rabin, the man who a few months later would sign the peace agreement with Arafat. But it was Rabin who sent his troops to "break bones" during the Palestinian **Intifada**. Willingly or otherwise, most Israelis supported their governments which occupied, dispossessed, repressed and suppressed more than a generation of Arabs in Palestine, Lebanon and Syria. Some of the most outspoken proponents of the continuation of those policies even use terminology unwittingly borrowed from the Nazi era. They use the Hebrew equivalent of *Lebensraum* (German for "living space" – a euphemism for occupation for the purposes of enlarging the territorial base).

It seems, therefore, that the Israeli sociopolitical psyche is traumatized by the Holocaust experience, in ways it neither admits to nor fully understands, but which make its coming to terms with equal relations with its neighbours – the original population of the Middle East – a problematic, if not impossible, process. The brutality of the Holocaust, its stark power relations, seem to have stamped a pattern of behaviour on Israeli society which makes dealing with its enemies difficult. As the Palestinians are captives in their own country, victims of Israeli policies, so are the Israelis captives of their own misconceptions, which in turn determine a vicious circle of spiralling atrocities. While for many years Israel could claim that it had no partner for peace, and thus justify its actions, this is no longer possible. Since the Sadat visit in 1989, and definitely since 1993 in Oslo, the possibility is there for Israel to abandon its military exploits and join the nations of the Middle East. Will the memory and trauma of the Holocaust help Israel to decide, or indeed prevent the only viable decision?

Bibliography

General Overview:

Arendt, Hannah – *The Origins of Totalitarianism;* Harcourt, Brace & World, New York 1968. A analytical study of modern totalitarian systems of government.

Dawidowicz, Lucy – *The War Against the Jews 1933-1945;* Penguin Books, London 1990, Bantam Books, New York, 1986. Crucial source book.

Dawidowicz, Lucy – *A Holocaust Reader;* Bantam Books, New York 1976.

Gilbert, Martin – *The Holocaust;* Fontana, London 1987, Henry Holt, New York 1985.

Gilbert, Martin – *The Macmillan Atlas of the Holocaust;* Macmillan, New York 1982.

Hilberg, Raul – *The Destruction of the European Jews;* Leicester University Press, London 1986, Holmes & Meyer, New York 1967. Crucial source book.

Kenrick, Donald & Gratton, Paxton – *The Destiny of Europe's Gypsies,* Basic Books, New York 1972. The best source book on the topic.

Mendelsohn, John (ed) – *The Holocaust;* Garland, New York 1982. 18 volumes of documentation, used in the Nurenberg trials.

Poliakov, Leon – *The History of Anti-Semitism,* 3 Vols; Oxford University Press, London 1985, Vanguard Press, New York 1965-1975. Analytical history of anti-semitism.

Detailed Studies:

Vago, Bela & Mosse, George (eds) – *Jews and Non-Jews in Eastern Europe, 1918-1945;* Wiley, New York 1974.

Bauman, Zigmunt – *Modernity and the Holocaust;* Polity Press, Cambridge 1989. An important sociological study of the Holocaust and the reactions to it.

Beit-Zvi, S B – *Post-Ugandian Zionism in the Crucible of the Holocaust* (Hebrew); Bronfman, Tel Aviv 1977. Crucial source book on the Zionist reaction to Nazism and the Holocaust.

Braham, Randolph – *The Politics of Genocide;* 2 Vols; CUP, New York 1981.

Cohen, Elie – *Human Behaviour in the Concentration Camps;* Free Association Books, London 1988, Norton, New York 1953. A psychoanalytical study of camp behaviour and effects.

Dobroazycki, Lucjan (ed) – *The Chronicle of the Lodz Ghetto 1941-1944;* Yale University Press, New Haven 1984. Important source book.

Ehrenburg, Ilya & Grossman, Vasily (eds) – *The Black Book;* Holocaust Library, New York 1981. Source book on the destruction within the USSR.

Feig, Konnilyn – *Hitler's Death Camps;* Holmes & Meyer, New York 1981. Crucial source book on the various extermination camps.

Friedman, Philip – *Martyrs and Fighters;* Frederick Praeger, New York 1954.

Gilbert, Martin – *Auschwitz and the Allies;* Mandarin, London 1991, Holt, Reinhart and Wilson, New York 1981. Analysis of the information available to the Allies, and their failure to bomb Auschwitz during 1944.

Gutman, Ysrael – *The Jews of Warsaw 1939-1945;* Indiana University Press, Bloomington 1982

Hilberg, Raul – *Perpetrators Victims Bystanders;* Limetree, London 1993, Harper Collins, New York 1992. An analytical study of the complex system which enabled the Holocaust.

Hilberg, Raul – *The Warsaw Diary of Adam Czerniakow;* Stein & Day, NY 1979. The diary of the Warsaw Judenrat leader, who committed suicide on the eve of deportation.

Hitler, Adolf – *Mein Kampf;* Hutchinson, London 1969.

Hoss, Rudolph – *Commandant in Auschwitz;* World Publishing Co., Cleveland 1959.

Levai, Eugene – *Black Book on the Martyrdom of Hungarian Jewry;* Central European Times Publishing Co., Zurich and Vienna 1948. Important source book on this topic.

Morse, Arthur – *While Six Millions Died;* Random House, New York 1967. A critical analysis of the role played by the US during the destruction years.

Muller, Filip – *Eyewitness Auschwitz;* Stein and Day, New York 1979. Vivid survivor account.

Poliakov, Leon & Sabille, Jacques – *Jews Under the Italian Occupation;* Paris, 1955.

Presser, Jacob – *The Destruction of the Dutch Jews;* Dutton, New York 1969.

Ringelblum, Emmanuel – *Notes on the Warsaw Ghetto;* McGraw-Hil, New York 1959. The notes by the Warsaw Ghetto historian, who died in 1944.

Trunk, Isiah – *Judenrat;* Macmillan, New York 1972. A crucial work, describing and analysing the activity and constraints of the Jewish Councils appointed by the Nazis.

Wasserstein, Bernard – *Britain and the Jews of Europe, 1935-1945;* Oxford University Press, London 1979. A critical study of the role played by Britain.

Wyman, David – *Paper Walls;* University of Mass. Press, Amherst 1968. A critique of US bodies failing to act during the war.

Haim Bresheeth
Indepedent film maker, lecturer in media studies and writer on Middle Eastern affairs. Son of Holocaust survivors. Israeli socialist living in London.

Thanks to my parents.

Stuart Hood
Writer, novelist, translator, documentary film maker and ex-BBC executive, ex-professor in film at the Royal College of Art. Honorary member of ANPI (National Association of Italian Partisans).
Author of *Introducing Fascism* and *Introducing Marquis de Sade.*

Litza Jansz
Illustrator, designer, animator, independent film maker producing and directing films for C4 and the BBC. Lecturer in Media Studies and Animation.
Illustrator of *Introducing Fascism* and *Introducing Semiotics.*

A big thanks to Norma for her patience, support, expertise and advice throughout the project.
Thanks to Natty for advice and asylum.

With thanks to the Weiner Library and the Imperial War Museum.

Typesetting by Norma Spence

Index